LEADERSHIP SERIES

How to Conduct Win-Win Performance Appraisals

Written by Karen McKirchy
Edited by National Press Publications

NATIONAL PRESS PUBLICATIONS
6901 West 63rd Street • P.O. Box 2949 • Shawnee Mission, Kansas 66201-1349
1-800-258-7248 • 1-913-432-7757

National Seminars endorses nonsexist
language. In an effort to make this handbook
clear, consistent and easy to read, we've used
"he" throughout the odd-numbered chapters and
"she" throughout the even-numbered chapters.
The copy is not intended to be sexist.

This handbook is designed to provide an instructional
view of performance appraisals. It *is not* intended to
provide legal advice or counsel. It is important that you
consult with your attorney or personnel office before
actually addressing specific issues with an employee.

How to Conduct Win-Win Performance Appraisals

Printed in the United States of America

1 2 3 4 5 6 7 8 9 10

ISBN 1-55852-128-3

TABLE of CONTENTS

INTRODUCTION

Whether you are a supervisor, manager, or team leader, your people must grow, and that growth can be managed! It is important to understand that you do not get paid for what you do; you get paid for what your people do. The performance appraisal provides you with the opportunity to direct your employees' attention to the things that really matter. You're judged on the results you're able to achieve, but these results must be achieved through others.

This book will help you achieve better results by developing an honest, productive relationship with your people. It tells you not only what you should do, but also how you should do it.

An effective appraisal system takes two forms: formal performance appraisals and ongoing performance feedback appraisals. During formal performance appraisals, a specific time is set aside to meet with the employee and a formal record of this meeting becomes part of the employee's permanent personnel record. Ongoing performance feedback appraisals, on the other hand, are useful for behavior modification and ongoing communication. They set the stage for many of the issues that will be addressed in the formal, sit-down performance appraisal. The techniques we discuss are applicable to both types of appraisals. However, the focus of this book is on the dynamics of the successful formal, sit-down performance appraisal.

You'll learn how to establish a work climate that is conducive to productive performance appraisals, and be able to initiate and maintain positive communications with your employees about their work performance. You'll also learn to set expectations and produce better results.

HOW TO CREATE "SAME-SIDE-OF-THE-DESK" THINKING

The General Objectives of Performance Appraisals

Performance appraisals involve setting goals, judging the results achieved and creating performance criteria that can be met and measured over and over again for each of your employees' job description. You should focus on three things:

- Focus on performance, not personalities.

- Focus on valid, concrete, relevant issues rather than subjective emotions and feelings.

- Reach agreement on what the employee is going to improve in his performance and what you are going to do.

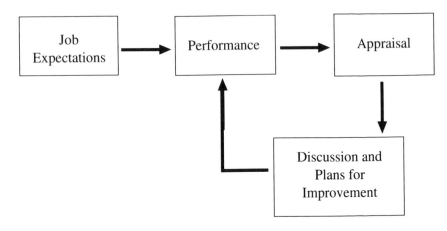

The Appraisal Cycle

In conducting performance appraisals, you need to make it very clear that *your objective is performance, not personality* issues. This is a big step towards "same-side-of-the-desk" thinking. Together, you and your employee both look at what can be done to solve performance problems.

> ## HOW NOT TO DO IT
>
> **Supervisor**: You are always late. Some people in your department think you are lazy.
>
> **Employee**: I am not lazy. If you think that, you don't understand me at all.

By implying that the employee is lazy, personality issues, emotions and defenses immediately take over. Saying that the employee is always late isn't quantified. Instead, to make it a factual performance issue, it must be measurable 5 days out of the last 15, for example.

HOW TO DO IT

Supervisor: You need to focus on being here on time. Some of your customers call you at 8:00 AM, and you're not here to take care of them.

Employee: You are right. I can't get the same level of sales from them as from my other customers. Maybe that's the reason.

Supervisor: Is there anything I can do to help you?

By focusing on specific, often numeric or recorded information, the facts become the facts, rather than feelings. Facts can be addressed. Feelings escalate and become the foundation for self-justification, blame and continued poor performance.

HOW NOT TO DO IT

Supervisor: You are always late. You are never here when your key accounts call.

Employee: I haven't been late that much . . . *(Thinking . . . you just don't like me, so you are exaggerating)* Get off my back.

HOW TO DO IT

Supervisor: You have been late 10 of the last 30 days. You're missing key account calls.

Employee: I didn't realize it was that much! I'm always behind with my key accounts. That's probably why.

Supervisor: Is there anything I can do to help you?

Performance Appraisal Essentials

Be very clear in your communications. Use a 1-2-3 format:

1. Attempt to eliminate any misunderstandings.
2. Quantify specifically *what* is expected from the employee.
3. Describe exactly *when* it is expected.

The attitude you want to take is that you and the employee are partners in successful problem-solving.

HOW NOT TO DO IT

> **Supervisor**: This can't continue. If you don't change, there
> will be serious consequences.
>
> **Employee**: OK. I'll do better.

In this episode, you use threats but no measurement; you have
expectations with no consequences and specify no time frame when
action will be taken.

HOW TO DO IT

> **Supervisor**: This can't continue. Beginning tomorrow you are
> expected to be here by 8:00 to handle your job. If you
> are not here, I will give key accounts who call in to
> another representative. When your key accounts decline
> by 10%, your salary will be adjusted accordingly, and if
> we reach 20%, we will reassign your area to someone
> else.
>
> **Employee**: That's pretty harsh. I'm just a little late.
>
> **Supervisor**: No. You are missing key contact calls because
> you are a "little" late, as you call it.

These are the basic components of good performance communications. If you are successful in executing the basic components, you gain the following advantages:

- You are forced to assess and realize that an employee's poor performance could be the result of inadequate management. Your attention is focused on what you need to do and say. Once you realize the role you play, the steps you take can focus the relationship between you and your employee, helping it to function productively on an adult-to-adult level.

- You provide employees with feedback on their performance, enabling them to learn what's expected to become a more successful member of your team.

- You can recognize and reinforce good performance and set goals for the future. When goals are set by the employee, there is more motivation to achieve those goals.

- You are given another tool for helping employees solve problems, one of your most important tools . . . the tool that gets results!

The performance appraisal process provides useful feedback, helping you and your company optimize human assets. New goals and objectives are agreed upon and work teams can be restructured for maximum efficiency. The development of your department must reflect the interests, abilities and motivations of the employees who comprise it; otherwise, achieving objectives will be nearly impossible. These goals emerge through the "same-side-of-the-desk" thinking of a well-planned performance system.

The performance appraisal serves as the basis for you and your employee to strengthen your relationship and become a solid team, two adults working toward a common, agreed-upon goal. It forces you to look at your own actions to see what supervision the employee requires for better performance. Your job is to identify quickly the techniques that work with individual employees and adjust your own style to get the maximum productivity from each of your employees.

Leadership, Your Style and Performance Improvement

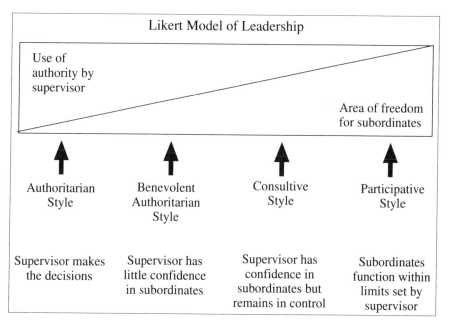

Look at each end of this chart, beginning on the left side. Some employees cannot deal with too much independent decision-making. They need a supervisor to decide and direct their work, using an authoritarian style.

AUTHORITARIAN

Employee: I don't know how to handle the call to ABC Company. They never respond, and I never get a sale with them. I just don't know what to do.

Supervisor: Handle them as we handled that call with XYZ Company. You offered to come over to see their operation. They liked that, and that opened the door for you. Call them right now.

Employee: You are right. That's what I need to do!

PARTICIPATIVE

Supervisor: What problem do you see handling the DEF Company account?

Employee: I can't get them to make a commitment. We're just one of a number of companies calling on them right now. They think our product is a commodity, and they want to buy only on price.

Supervisor: How do you think you should handle it?

Employee: I would like to invite them over for a tour of our facility to show them how advanced we are in quality management. I think we can distinguish ourselves from the competition in that area and show them the value added with our products . . . that there really is a difference, not only with our products but also with our people.

Supervisor: That's a fine idea. How can I help?

You'll notice that in the last example the supervisor lets the employee solve his own problem (participative). In contrast, in the first example (authoritarian), direct commands are given for the employee to execute. The supervisor knows that the employee will execute them well but that he has trouble seeing the right thing to do on his own, so the supervisor tells the employee in no uncertain terms (authoritarian) what should be done.

Your leadership style must change with different issues and different employees. This is not the same as being wishy-washy or a constantly changing person whom no one can get a fix on. It means that you carefully consider what will work for each individual and situationally apply a technique or a series of techniques to accomplish the objective. This does not mean bearing the entire responsibility for your subordinate's performance yourself. The employee has equal responsibility. But it's your job, as a leader, to see that he has been provided with everything necessary to meet his job responsibilities.

When employees hear performance feedback from a well-done appraisal session, they have real, solid information to act on. Without such information, they're guessing and their record usually indicates inadequacies. Time spent guessing is wasted, unproductive time. You can't afford to have your people work in a "guessing" mode, and neither can your company.

HOW NOT TO DO IT

Supervisor: So, let's close by focusing on the fact that you
need to make more good sales calls each day.

Employee: *(after the meeting)* My supervisor talked about how
I needed to make more good calls each day. But what's a
"good" call? I guess I'll just make more calls.
Obviously, the company is only interested in the number
of calls, not how well they're done or the results. I'll just
fill up my call sheet . . .

You can see in the above example that the supervisor's guidance is
incomplete. What really constitutes a "good" sales call? The employee
may increase the number of calls, but is left guessing how to improve the
quality or the results.

Positive Performance Feedback

Sometimes when people think of performance appraisals, they think
only of the negative. While it is important to put out the most
threatening fires, giving positive feedback to employees is very
important. This is especially true when employees have just made a
difficult change. They need to know you're watching and recognizing
their work and that they're achieving results.

If you do have negative feedback to give, a well-known successful
technique, called "insertion," usually proves successful. First a positive
comment is made, then the negative feedback is "inserted" and a positive
comment finally closes. The overall effect on the employee is positive
while a negative concern still is being addressed. This technique is
especially useful with an employee who is trying, making progress, or
who just doesn't handle criticism well. It's not recommended where
stern warnings are required, however.

HOW TO DO IT

Supervisor: I really like the way you've taken control of the DEF account. *(Positive)*

Employee: Thank you. It felt good to finally get them as a regular customer.

Supervisor: The TUV account is causing a lot of problems. *(Negative)* We need to discuss what to do about it. You handled the ABC account well. *(Positive)* How can we use what we learned on ABC to solve the problems with TUV?

The performance appraisal process helps determine where an employee is in his development and helps the company better deploy the skill sets of its employees to achieve the business objectives. Here are a few tips you'll find helpful. *Remember: real-time feedback motivates!*

- The time to correct an employee's mistake is when it happens. Don't allow an error to become a habit.

- The performance appraisal process should be a summary of the day-to-day realizations the employee and you share.

- The magic isn't in the appraisal form . . . it's in the people trying to work together to create a better future.

- Properly conducted, the performance appraisal process provides as much relationship improvement as performance improvement.

The pace of business today is hectic and will likely continue as the trend toward downsizing/rightsizing continues and world-wide competitive pressures increase. The time to talk about good and bad performance is when it happens, when the issues are clear and not influenced by the rush of memories.

Employees become motivated when they feel you are there with them, caring, coaching and understanding the events that occur. You want to stop something before it becomes larger, so by dealing with it quickly you can get it out of the way and move on to other matters, like increasing productivity. By dealing with things as they happen, you also avoid festering feelings.

The Formal, Sit-Down Performance Appraisal

If you realize you have failed to change your employee's behavior through daily interaction, you can use the formal, sit-down performance appraisal to finally get your point across.

Properly handled, the formal, sit-down performance appraisal becomes a summary of observations as well as a solid platform for new understanding of how to achieve the best results possible.

Once you observe less than optimal results, it's time to revisit your employee's job description. It describes accepted expectations and offers a format for discussing where performance has slipped; the employee can then modify his actions and you can provide appropriate help. An honest discussion of shortfalls and performance results should refocus both you and your employee. The form itself is only a guideline to help the conversation focus productively.

The magic comes when the two people communicate, break through their problems and obstacles, celebrate their success and plan for more. The employee in this framework feels a part of the process rather than a victim of it. The relationship between team members also can improve.

Performance improvement often follows naturally because you took time to refocus your employee's personal pride. Employees are normally highly motivated with a desire to please. Use this to your advantage in directing their actions and building your relationship with them.

2

LEGAL ISSUES

Employment Law

Uniform Guidelines on Employee Selection 1978 is the controlling federal law in the area of performance appraisals. Your company's performance appraisal system is central to nearly all personnel processes: hiring, promotion, demotion, transfer, salary, selection for training, etc. This book will not focus on all the legal ramifications; you need to talk to your legal counsel about such matters. Most well-run companies will train you in-depth in these areas because they hold much of the legal liability. However, your performance reviews must be workable, equitable, ongoing and as objective as possible, for you and your organization are expected to follow and meet all legal requirements. Lack of knowledge or ignorance of the law is no excuse for violations.

Your performance appraisal must have **no adverse impact** on any of the areas covered by the law, such as employees':

- race

- sex

- religion

- national origin

- age

- handicapped status

These are the major areas covered, but they may not describe all the areas protected by law when you read this. Consult your company's training guide or your personnel manager about any questions. You must understand that if a member of any "protected" group is adversely impacted, the performance appraisal practice is illegal. All performance appraisal practices must contain *measuring standards*. What does this mean?

Special Tip: Questions about antidiscrimination laws and the current enforcement policies of the Equal Employment Opportunity Commission can be directed to agency experts through a nationwide free information hotline. Dial (800) USA-EEOC. Calls made from a touch-tone phone will be answered by a recording, but you can talk to a specialist by dialing "2" after you hear the recording.

Measurement Standards

Measuring standards are valid when you can:

1. prove content validity — a person must be able to perform this task to do her job.

2. prove construct validity — you must show the relationship between rating scores and traits or skills needed on the job.

3. prove criterion-related validity — you must show the relationship between rating scores and measure of job performance.

In other words, in order to be legal, a certain skill must be shown to be a valid, true and necessary requirement of the job. Discrimination against protected groups is allowable as long as the discriminating variable is legitimately related to the requirements of the work situation. For example, if the next level job on the factory floor demands the ability to lift 75 pounds above waist height, and a wheelchair-bound employee cannot perform this task, it is acceptable not to promote that person to that job.

You must be able to consistently observe the employee performing the assigned tasks. Your rating criteria must be the same for all employees of the same grade/class/group. But be careful: using numerical scores increases an organization's liability to validate them. Just because something is expressed in numbers does not automatically make it legal.

Another important aspect to consider is the employee's right to privacy. Employees must have complete access to their personnel files, but others should have controlled access. These records must be accurate, relevant and current. Discuss with your personnel department any questions you have in these areas, but keep in mind that job-relatedness and fairness are the two controlling principles whenever you put something in writing.

Substantial performance, or even average performance, should not be described in such a way that the employee believes her performance is better than it is. You do a great disservice to your employee and your team when you praise what's less than adequate performance. Besides, you flirt with performance collapse. Employees soon lose confidence in you, their trust sags and respect falls.

Performance must be described *accurately* and must be based on *documentation*. If an employee is terminated for poor performance, but previous reviews were either good or vague, the employee may have grounds for a wrongful discharge lawsuit. All performance appraisal feedback as well as any other employee communications must be free of sexual innuendo or sexual harassment.

WARNING! Be careful of rating subjective qualities: attitude, cooperation, enthusiasm, initiative. Subjective ratings are difficult for you or your company to defend in court. Quantifiable areas such as deadlines met, calls made, items produced, quota achieved, etc., are much easier to defend and are more productive for you and your employee.

3

CLARIFYING NEEDS

Employee Needs

Everyone has needs in the workplace. Here are the most important needs from your employee's viewpoint.

1. To know how/what he is doing relative to your expectations and the company's goals.

2. To understand the following:

   - The criteria to be used in the performance appraisal.
   - How his performance will be measured (against which standard).
   - Who will do the appraisal.

- When the appraisal will be done.
- What feedback he will get.
- If he can give input to the process and when.
- What assistance the company will provide in improving performance.
- What the rewards are for above average performance.

3. To be listened to in the following areas:

- How things are going on the job in general.
- Any specific problems he is experiencing.
- What you, as supervisor, can do to make his job less frustrating and him more effective.
- What the employee thinks he is doing well and suggested areas for improvement.

4. To receive helpful, constructive feedback.

5. To be treated with dignity and respect.

6. To feel that someone cares.

There are several other factors to consider when looking at the relationship between employee performance appraisals and your employee's needs:

1. The employee's desire to be evaluated varies both within each individual and from individual to individual over time. An individual who believes his performance is good is less concerned about the opinions of others regarding performance. An individual who is success-oriented in his performance is more interested in feedback than one who fears failure.

2. The anticipation of being evaluated is threatening. Therefore, hostility is often directed toward performance appraisers. An employee often views an evaluation as an occasion when he lacks control of his fate, and he is frequently apprehensive and anxious. Individuals with low self-esteem are more apt to feel threatened than those with high self-esteem. Negative reactions to criticism often occur if ongoing support is not available from you.

3. The more an individual is able to influence his evaluator, the more likely he is to accept an evaluation as his own evaluation. The relationship between a supervisor and his associates determines whether the latter accept the former's ratings. An expert appraiser's opinions are more likely to be accepted than those of a non-expert. Your staff is more likely to accept your ratings if they like and respect you, and an individual is more likely to accept evaluations that are similar to those he has received from other appraisers.

Employer's Needs

Employers have needs, too! Since the employee is an asset of the company, the employer needs to regularly review and direct productively the contributions its employees make toward achieving the company's objectives. As a manager or supervisor, you must focus yourself on the needs of your organization, including:

1. Performance appraisals that help control quality, performance and output.

2. A system that identifies both individual employee and departmental training needs.

3. Necessary information for manpower and organizational planning.

4. Recommendations that reinforce or suggest modifications to the employee selection process.

5. A performance system that improves employee morale and offers recognition and reward for above average performance.

6. An opportunity to talk about how to develop particular employees.

7. Time to talk about the job and what needs to be done to improve.

8. A chance to motivate, teach and coach. This area is often not clearly recognized by either employer or employee.

A mutuality develops when you pay attention to your employee's needs, and a true sense of respect emerges when your own and the organization's needs are shared with the employee.

4

THE PERFORMANCE APPRAISAL SYSTEM

Four Types of Appraisal Systems

The following section lists different types of performance appraisal systems and some of the advantages of each. Carefully read the description of each type of system. You will find ideas you can use, no matter what style your company currently follows. Four different types of appraisal systems are:

- Self-Directed Work Teams
- Peer Appraisal Systems
- Self-Rating Systems Combined with Formal Performance Appraisal
- Other Performance Systems

Self-Directed Work Teams

Overview: In this model, the performance appraisal is the primary vehicle for communicating business strategy to employees. Each team has a family of critical measures linked to measures of performance that, in turn, constitute the overall business strategy. These measures are revised annually.

Description: Performance measures usually fall into the following groups:

- Quality

- Financial – cost and revenue considerations

- Timeliness

- Productivity/efficiency

Associated with each measure are three criteria: a long-term goal, short-term goals and the minimum standards of performance.

Teams usually:

- Identify behaviors that have the greatest impact on performance.

- Measure behavior and create specific feedback on team performance compared to the goal. Employees keep track of their own performance. Weekly and monthly team meetings are held to identify problems and work through solutions.

- Rely on managers who are trained to reinforce desired behavior as it occurs, not just once or twice a year.

Individual employee performance goals center primarily on learning and development. Goals for an individual might be to improve communication or build problem-solving skills. General actions to achieve these goals might be taking on more leadership responsibilities in meetings (communication) or serving on a taskforce (problem-solving). Specific tactics might include working on different communication or problem-solving techniques.

Personal contribution to the team's goals might include: quality improvement, cost reduction, or improvements in customer service. Team goals clarify the role of the workgroup. Workgroups are charged with the responsibility to accomplish a "family of measures," five to ten key measures of performance that the team must monitor, control and improve.

In summary, the self-directed work team performance appraisal system is one type of system used by companies that utilize work teams. This systems allows you to conduct short, ongoing, informal reviews as well as formal reviews every quarter. It provides the freedom to structure the review in light of individual and team needs. It is not just a paperwork exercise but real, ongoing communication with no once-a-year surprises.

Peer Appraisal

Overview: Sometimes you may use this technique to gain additional information, especially when using work teams.

Description: The employee is reviewed by her peers. Feedback is collected from team members, compiled by the appraiser and used in combination with a more traditional appraisal form.

Advantages: A well-rounded view of performance can be gained by combining a variety of perspectives. It also builds peer accountability.

Disadvantages: Veracity and commitment of your employees. Helping them feel good about the process takes time. Here are some guidelines to making a peer evaluation system work:

1. Start small. Don't try to get everyone to appraise everyone. Begin with one or two peer evaluations. Sometimes the employee picks her own peer evaluators.

2. Protect the confidentiality of all peer ratings. Truthfulness and honest feedback increase when peers know their specific insights will not be exposed. Your employee needs to know "how" she is perceived by the team, not necessarily the specifics.

3. When peers know that performance and income potential come from these ratings, it is very tempting to write favorable reviews. No one wants to take food from someone else. It's important that you deemphasize punishment, emphasize positive criticism and keep everyone focused on team success.

4. Do not abdicate your managerial responsibilities to the peer review. The peer review offers valuable information that should support and affirm the key points you choose to appraise. If you are out of step with an employee's peer reviews, rethink your perceptions.

Self-Rating Systems Combined with Formal Performance Appraisal

Overview: Self-rating creates a participative approach to the traditional appraisal method. Employees rate their performance and then review it with you. This is the method we will expand upon in an upcoming section, "The Employee Self-Analysis." You can change the rating to reflect the true situation if the employee has rated herself too high or too low. Responsibility for the performance appraisal is delegated to the employee. This method treats people like adults. Your role truly becomes one of counselor, teacher and coach.

Description: Ninety percent of all self-appraisals rate employees at or below what you would! This high percentage makes the method viable. Your role becomes one of praising, encouraging, and being generally positive to the employee. The employee comes away with a better self-image.

If an employee rates herself correctly, your role becomes one of confirmation and reinforcement. This leads naturally into a "Where do we go from here?" attitude, opening up exploration of further development and improvement.

Ten percent of employees will rate themselves higher than the manager does. Half of them believe their performance is that good. This calls for a response from you. These employees usually aren't trying to fight about their rating; they simply have a different perception. The other half are really troubled, however. They have inflated opinions of themselves, and they sometimes argue. These are the employees who are not happy under any performance appraisal system.

Advantages: Self-rating stands up well in court defenses. Fewer cases go to court when the employee participates in her own performance appraisal than when appraisals are completed only by supervisors.

Other Performance Systems

You'll probably find one of the following to be the basis for your company's performance appraisal form. Each of the major types is briefly reviewed below.

1. *Rating Scales:* Behaviorally anchored rating scales are charted. Key issues are targeted and measured. You sample behavior over the long term and do not rely on short-range judgments and impressions. Such scales reveal the complex behaviors that contribute to successful performance.

2. *Forced Rank Comparisons:* These are based on the selection of one statement from three to five alternatives that the appraiser thinks most accurately describes employee behavior. Each statement is weighted; therefore, employees with higher scores are deemed to be better than employees with lower scores.

3. *Critical Incident:* The appraiser records critical incidents and stores them for communication during the appraisal. This method is generally viewed as ineffective because the feedback should be given at the time the incident occurred to be effective.

4. *Free-Form Essay:* This system usually consists of a description, in the appraiser's words, of the employee's overall performance, including quantity and quality of work, job know-how, and ability to get along with other employees. The appraiser lists both the employee's good points and shortcomings.

Why Do Some Supervisors Fail to Conduct Performance Appraisals?

There are many reasons why you may fail to discuss your employees' performance. You may avoid dealing with your employees because the appraisal form is too complicated. A more subtle form of avoidance involves discussing only the positive aspects, never digging into any negative aspects. Why does avoidance occur?

1. Some people fear the possibility of disagreement and confrontation, as well as accumulation of hostility over past events. Once an argument starts, supervisors feel they have to win. So do the employees. Usually, neither wins.

2. Lack of interpersonal and interviewing skills is another common reason for avoiding employee performance reviews. If you do not know the techniques for directing the appraisal interview, you're not likely to look forward to it.

3. The fear of making matters worse by talking about the review.

4. Effective appraisal interviews depend in part on establishing limited, attainable objectives. If your organization's forms are too complex, they take over the process. Hundreds of items on a form do not lend themselves to pursuing a limited number of objectives. They make it difficult to even start!

5. Who else looks at the forms and why? A superior's review can influence what you do. This reality may overshadow real communication and make the process seem phony.

6. The fact that an employee's work is favorable does not automatically ensure a promotion, but employees sometimes think so. This mistaken notion often results in disappointment for the employee. When you cannot deliver a promotion, you may avoid an employee review for fear of losing that employee.

7. When performance and salary reviews are combined, the overriding message becomes dollars. Performance appraisal and salary review are not very compatible, and combining them leads to less effective and often messy encounters. Some people use separate sessions, but the time to do both slips away.

The performance appraisal is your most effective management tool. Many managers fail to view their people as a business resource and, therefore, fail to manage them accordingly. Business decisions are made every day to invest money in fixing up the "old one" rather than buying a "new one." Your staff should be viewed the same way. It may cost $30,000 or more to replace a professional employee but only $15,000 to $20,000 to retrain or modify a current employee's behavior.

A very profitable business decision is made when you learn to focus your energies on performance appraisals, spending time to help with employee performance. You must accept full responsibility for the success or failure of your human resources, the same way you have accepted full responsibility for non-human resources (machinery, deadlines, finances, materials, facilities, products, etc.).

5

THE PERFORMANCE INTERVIEW

An Overview

The actual performance interview is not the beginning or the end of anything. It is the middle step in a continuing, repetitive cycle with the content of each discussion changing.

Your first step is to define the job. Don't be content with a job description that is supplied to you. Look at it carefully to see if it truly relates to your department, your company and your goals TODAY! Ask yourself, "What is it I really want my employee to do?" And if there's more than a 10% change from what's written in the job description, rewrite it! Better yet, write it with your employee.

Your second step is to communicate the job effectively to the employee, leveling on what is expected. This goes beyond handing your employee written job specs. It goes to the heart of what is expected and, if appropriate, the when and the how.

The third step in the appraisal cycle is keeping a performance log on each employee and updating it frequently. The performance log contains the date, the event, the action taken, the result and the follow-up information on each employee. These are primarily incident reports, including progress reports where you evaluate work in progress. Pick a time period each week to update these logs. It is necessary not only to document extraordinary events but also to make summary entries. Stick to the facts in your entries. Personal feelings or opinions will not be helpful to you later.

The actual performance appraisal should not be too extensive; after all, everyone fails periodically. The purpose of the appraisal is not to communicate all your judgments. You must learn to limit yourself, covering what's possible. You control the appraisal. What you want to accomplish determines how you plan and conduct an appraisal.

- Set your objectives.
- Determine what will be talked about.
- Keep the interview on track.

By keeping the interview on track, you get the employee to want to improve his performance. The key to successful appraisals is being able to answer "yes" to each of these questions:

- Does the employee know what is expected?

- Have you developed objectives for the interview based on your desired results?

- Will you control the appraisal interview and not let an appraisal form do it?

- Have you developed a strategy for the appraisal interview?

- Do you have the necessary skills to do what you want to do?

If you cannot answer "yes" to each of these questions, you are not ready to discuss performance with your employee.

The Appraisal Form

Before you can become proficient in each aspect of conducting a successful performance appraisal, you must understand how your company expects the performance appraisal to be used. After understanding your company's policy, consider the following topics.

1. Make sure the form serves your needs as well as the needs of the employee you will be rating. Normally, forms cover too much. If the form is too overwhelming, it's not helpful. Further, when a form deals with attitudes and other abstract behavior, how do you get objective measurements? Abstract behavior is not as objective an assessment as "five days late in the last thirty-day period"; yet it is often treated as such. How will you keep from having a negative impact on performance when using the form?

2. The performance appraisal form is not your only basis for employee appraisal. Don't fill out the form and send it in without consulting the employee, but don't change the form after discussing it with the employee.

3. Everyone should view and use appraisals professionally. Appraisals are personal and privileged information.

4. Appraisal forms should call for objective data on the employee's performance. Performance should be rated as "satisfactory" or "unsatisfactory" with a space for comments. You and the

employee should work on the form together. Each of you should review a blank form in preparation for the meeting and then complete the form in the meeting, utilizing joint discussion without preconceptions.

This approach usually results in the most successful appraisals. You are free to conduct a purposeful appraisal interview without the constrictions of the form. If a form is required, use it. But don't let the form limit a meaningful performance discussion with your employee.

Preparing for the Performance Appraisal

The following points offer you a step-by-step method for analyzing employee behavior. By looking carefully at your employee's performance and writing down specifics to discuss, you will feel prepared. This helps build your own confidence and results in a more positive experience for both you and the employee.

The basis for this preparation is a review of your performance log. Review each incident report and progress report you filed. Significant problems should not wait for discussion in a formal review. You don't want to approach the formal performance review with negative surprises. This documentation focuses you on actual performance and experience rather than personality issues. As a result, you'll be more likely to remain objective.

1. Formulate positive behavior goals for your employee. During performance appraisals, it's easy to come from the negative point of view, i.e., listing the things that are not being done, etc. *It is better to ask for more of something than less of something.* Express yourself in terms of what is needed. Use a positive rather than a negative approach. For example, the statement "You are always late" needs to be changed to "You need to be on time." You may think it's a small change, but, taken all together, such statements can send very powerful messages.

HOW NOT TO DO IT
You are never on time.

HOW TO DO IT
You need to be here on time every day.

HOW NOT TO DO IT
You're rigid.

HOW TO DO IT
You need to be more flexible.

HOW NOT TO DO IT
You're too fussy.

HOW TO DO IT
You need to learn to distinguish between what's important and what's not important on the job.

2. Identify what's needed to improve the employee's performance. In what ways should he function more effectively? Determine whether addressing the problem is worth your time. If it's unimportant, you waste your time, the employee's time and the company's resources on an area where the return is not satisfactory. This is not good business.

3. Concentrate on the causes of the problem, not the symptoms. The solution must be related to the problem or it will be ineffective.

   Consult the following checklist:

   - Identify "nonperformance"
   - Determine if it is worth the time required to change nonperformance to performance
   - Does the employee know that the performance is not satisfactory?
   - Does the employee clearly understand what he is supposed to do and when?
   - Are there any obstacles that are beyond the employee's control?
   - Does the employee know how to do the job?
   - Does a negative result exist if the employee does not perform?
   - Have you removed rewards for your employee's nonperformance?
   - Could the employee do the task if he wanted to?

4. Collect information without making judgments by talking to the employee. Then you can help him discover what to do differently so that the results will change. Remember, you must identify the *behavior* that is causing the problem.

5. Make sure the employee knows there is a problem. Identify both the *specific* behavior changes you want your employee to make and *what the employee would have to do to* convince you the problem has been solved.

HOW TO DO IT

Supervisor *(thinking)*: Martha never listens, and she always seems to misunderstand directions. My goal is to have her listen and understand what I ask her to do. The specific things Martha will have to do to convince me she has accomplished this goal are:
- Doing things the way I ask her to do them, unless she checks with me first.
- Asking me for clarification if she does not understand.
- Repeating back to me the instruction, confirming her understanding.

---

6. Identify success areas. You must know where the employee is performing effectively and provide *specific* examples in each area. This cannot be emphasized enough. It is important to show positive performance examples as well as negative ones. If necessary, identify the specific consequences that will occur if the employee does not take action.

7. Review background information. It is helpful to know the employee's length of service with the company, the current projects the employee is working on, the date of the employee's last promotion, the employee's educational and experiential background, etc.

In summary, don't sit down with your employee until you have covered each of the above areas using your performance log on that employee, a record of the employee's attendance, the employee's personnel file, the employee's job description, and the job and career objectives drawn up in your last performance appraisal with your employee as reference. Then you are prepared.

Defining Job Expectations

Earlier we touched on job descriptions and their importance to the appraisal process. In preparing for the appraisal, you must examine the existing job description. What is its focus in the following areas?

- Customer satisfaction
- Economic health of the company
- Innovation
- Quality
- Productivity
- Human resources
- Organizational climate

List your own job expectations. Decide what you really expect this person to do on the job in the areas of:

- Objectives
- Projects
- Authority
- Priority
- Scheduling
- Results/standards of performance

What things do *you* value the most?

Appraise performance, not expectations. What are the employee's major strengths and weaknesses? What personal characteristics or habits block greater achievement? What's ahead for this person? Why?

Thought must be given at this point to how each of the above areas will be addressed in the appraisal interview with the employee. If each area is addressed, will it be too much for the employee to handle in one sitting? Which areas are the most important and how will they be covered?

Be conscious of the following tendencies and try to avoid them as you prepare to assess your employee:

Trait Assessment: Too much attention to certain characteristics that have nothing to do with the job or are difficult to measure blind us to more important traits.

Overemphasis: Too much emphasis on favorable or unfavorable performance of one or two tasks could lead to an unbalanced evaluation of the overall employee contribution.

Bias/Prejudice: Things that have nothing to do with performance such as race, religion, education, family background, age, handicapped status and/or sex do not belong in the evaluation.

False Reliance: Relying on impressions rather than the facts is unfair.

Misplaced Accountability: Holding the employee responsible for factors beyond his control is unrealistic.

Concentrate on performance measured against mutually understood expectations.

Asking the Employee to Meet – The Personal Touch

Your primary objective is to prepare the employee for a meaningful discussion with you. Don't have your secretary or another associate carry the invitation, and don't send a memo. When you ask personally, you have control over the entire process. You don't have to worry about another layer complicating communications. The personal touch is an important component you want to capitalize on at this point, and you want to begin the entire interaction on a positive, personal note.

- Don't combine the meeting itself with the invitation. Give the employee time to organize his thoughts so his feedback is more helpful to the process. Without sufficient time to prepare, people are normally reactionary and can become resentful.

- Don't underinform or overinform your employee of the details needed for a successful meeting.

- Don't be ambiguous; be clear. Ambiguity can result in anxiety. Anxiety can be counterproductive to good communication.

- Don't say too much or get dragged into answering questions that should be part of the appraisal interview.

- Don't mock the process by making jokes. You'll lose your credibility and any hope of achieving worthwhile objectives.

- Don't arrange the meeting when you are upset or angry.

The best way to ask an employee to meet is to approach him privately. Explain the purpose of the meeting and how you would like him to prepare. This is very important. Suggest that the employee prepare for the meeting by thinking of things he is doing well and areas that need improvement. The employee should also be asked to come prepared to discuss:

1. Job performance issues since the last review
2. Personal career objectives
3. Problems or concerns about the present job
4. Goals for improving performance and productivity

Finally, ask the employee to think about things you can do to make things better. This also is important. It sends a message that you want to hear the employee's input. It shows that you think of the appraisal as a two-way street, that you and the employee are a team and that you'll do your part. You might want to photocopy the list on page 40 as a tool your employee can use to prepare for his appraisal meeting.

HOW TO DO IT

Supervisor: *(to employee when no one is near)* I'd like to arrange a time to meet with you to review your work performance. Everyone in the office will be scheduled soon.

Employee: Okay . . .

Supervisor: I'm going to prepare for this meeting by writing down some of the things you have been doing really well and some of the areas where you can improve . . . I'd like you to prepare for the meeting by doing the same. First think about the things you are doing well. Then concentrate on the areas where you feel you could improve.

Employee: I can do that.

Supervisor: Also, I'd like you to think about areas where I could help make your job less frustrating and more satisfying for you. Okay?

Employee: Really? . . . I'll work on it.

Supervisor: Good. How's next Monday at 10:00 in my office?

Employee: That will be just fine.

Supervisor: Good. I'll see you then.

Questions the employee can ask as he prepares for his performance appraisal:

* What critical abilities does my job require?
* What were my special accomplishments during this appraisal period?
* What do I like about my job? What don't I like?
* What goals or standards didn't I meet?
* How could my supervisor help me?
* Is there anything that the organization or my supervisor is doing that is hindering my progress?
* How can I become more productive?
* Do I need more experience or training on my current job?
* What have I done since my last appraisal to prepare myself for more responsibility?
* What new goals or standards should be applied for the next appraisal period? Which old ones should be discarded?

Get organized and rehearse each step if you feel it's necessary in order to set the stage for the positive appraisal to follow.

The Employee Self-Analysis

A well-done performance appraisal requires the collaboration of you and your employee. The first step is to understand why the employee's self-analysis is important. Employees will appreciate your interest in their analysis because it's an expression of interest in them. By listening to your employee's view of his performance, you'll see things from another perspective. The self-analysis involves the employee in the process and helps cement a strong relationship between you. You'll get a much clearer picture of any differences in viewpoint, and you'll get valuable new information on strengths and areas needing improvement.

Communicate to your employee that the purpose is to:

- List areas of major responsibility and accountability.

- Identify areas where the employee thinks he is performing effectively.

- Identify areas for improvement and some specific things he could do to show improvement in each area.

- Help your employee chart realistic goals for the future.

Let the employee know you will be going through these steps also and that you will be comparing notes.

HOW TO DO IT

Supervisor: *(Begin by asking your employee to share his self-analysis)* Let's begin by talking about how you think you're doing on your job . . . . I'd like you to start by telling me several things you think you do particularly well. Please give me specific examples.

Employee: Okay . . . *(Very unsure)*

Supervisor: For instance, if I were asked to do a self-analysis, I'd mention my skill at prioritizing the work for my employees. To give an example, I would say, "I am very direct in outlining work assignments and when I expect things to be done." Do you understand what I mean and can you do this for me?

Employee: Yes. I relate well to the customer. *(Pause)* I think I'm flexible. *(Pause)* I also think I'm good at responding quickly in emergency situations. *(Pause looking serious and thoughtful)*

Supervisor: Good. I heard you mention three things. One, you're good at relating to the customers. Two, you're flexible. And three, you respond quickly in emergency situations. In what ways are you good at relating to customers? What are some of the things you do that lead you to conclude that this is a strong point?

Employee: Many customers are fearful when they come here. They are expecting to have a lot of trouble getting their problems resolved. I try to change the situation to a positive one by becoming someone they can relate to when they're here. I try to make sure they understand I'm listening to their troubles, and I give them assurance that something will be done.

Supervisor: *(Pausing to make sure the employee is finished)* I see. You're good at relating to customers because you reduce the fearfulness of the situation by becoming their ally, letting them know you care that their problem is solved; is that right?

Employee: Right. I think things like that are really important.

Supervisor: Very important. *(Pause)* Let's move to another area. You said you thought you were very good at emergencies. How did you mean that?

Employee: Do you remember the Davis case? There was a lot of tension in that situation. I wasn't nervous or scared during the entire episode.

Supervisor: Okay. Now let's identify several areas where you need to improve your work performance, those areas where you aren't performing as effectively as you might be. I'd like you to think about some of the specific things you'd actually do to improve in each area. *(Pause)* For example, one of the areas where I'd like to improve is handling conflicts between our department and other departments. One thing I know I could do to improve is to have the departments sit down together rather than meet with me one at a time. Do you understand?

Employee: Don't you think you're in a better position to tell me what areas I need to improve? You're familiar with my work, and you're my boss!

Supervisor: Yes, but for now I'd like to get some of your thoughts. I'll give you my suggestions later.

Employee: Okay. Let's see. The biggest thing, and I know you'll agree because you've reminded me of it, has to do with the customer service reports. I definitely think I can improve by writing up those reports when I finish each project. Another thing has to do with being better about getting here on time, especially when we're near the end of the month. *(Smiling)*

Supervisor: Yes . . . *(Pause)* So two areas where you could improve are being more conscientious about writing up customer service reports and getting to work on time. Anything else?

Employee: No, I can't think of anything right now.

Supervisor: Let's start with the first area, writing up customer service plans. What are some specific things you'd do to improve your performance in this area?

Employee: *(Pause)* Well, I put them off until the last minute and I usually end up scribbling my notes so they're hard for other people to read. *(Pause)* Because I'm rushing, I sometimes forget to record important information.

Supervisor: Okay, so to improve in this area you'd have to take the time to write notes that are legible and more complete?

Employee: Right. If they were legible, complete and on time, I would definitely say I had improved in this area.

Supervisor: *(Smiling)* All right. A little later, we'll talk about what you might actually do to achieve that goal. But now let's turn to the second area . . . arriving on time. What do you need to do to improve in that area?

Employee: *(Smiling)* That's easy! Just get to work on time.

Supervisor: Okay. But could you be just a little more specific? For example, if you got to work on time every day for the next ten days, would you say you had achieved your goal?

Employee: Oh . . . I see what you mean. *(Pause)* Uh . . . I guess now I arrive just a few minutes late about once a week. I guess I'd say that if I cut that down to being late only once a month I'd have achieved the goal.

In this scenario you see that a give-and-take, cooperative tone has been established, helping the employee look at both the positive and the negative aspects of performance.

6

UNDERSTANDING MOTIVATION

Three Theories of Motivation

What is motivation? Is it what you do to get others to do something you want them to do? Is it something that happens inside an individual that gets her to do something?

One theory of motivation holds that humans direct their actions to satisfy their own needs. Once a need is satisfied, it no longer motivates. Abraham H. Maslow, an often quoted author on the subject, categorizes needs as follows:

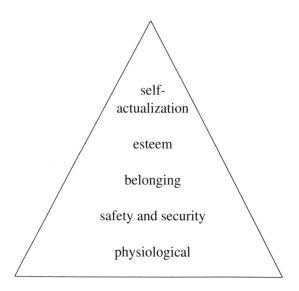

Supervisors determine at what level of need an employee is operating, and then ensure that elements in the workplace exist to satisfy those needs. Long conversations are often the way to understand what is going on in the employee's head.

Another way of looking at employee motivation is Theory X versus Theory Y, a concept advanced by Douglas McGregor. Theory X assumes people hate work, are not ambitious, are not responsible and prefer to be told what to do. Theory X managers believe people work only as long as they are watched, must be told specifically what to do and how to do it, and must be closely controlled until they do it. Theory Y managers, on the other hand, push authority down, assuming employees have a natural interest and willingness to work and do well at their jobs. These managers seek out ideas from their employees, looking for better ways of doing things.

Another noted behavior scientist, Frederick Herzberg, performed research on motivation, identifying satisfaction and dissatisfaction factors among workers. He found achievement to be the strongest employee motivator. Small achievements act as motivators, which cause people to achieve even more. According to Herzberg, the second strongest motivator is recognition. One effective way to increase productivity, for example, is to provide opportunities for achievement, giving the supervisor more opportunities to reward and recognize.

Unfortunately, most supervisors spend a lot of time convincing employees that the good work they produce is normal – that what they achieve is somehow expected and what they are paid to do! Recognition takes numerous forms beyond raises, bonuses or promotions. A major form of recognition is the positive things managers say to their achieving employees! Good supervision is recognizing the runners in the race who haven't won but are running better than they did before. So what can you do?

- Get out from behind your desk so you can discover more occurrences of achievement. Catch your employees doing something good.

- Recognize achievement immediately, the minute you become aware of it.

- Acknowledge that lesser degrees of failure are achievements; recognize them.

- Find more ways to show appreciation.

When you hire someone, you rent her behavior. When you are supervising someone, you direct and modify this behavior (not the person) in order to achieve the company's goals. Your goal is to avoid self-destructive behavior on both your part and the employee's part.

Communication Basics

The major reason for performance problems is lack of direction and lack of feedback . . . in other words, lack of effective communication. You are responsible for making sure your message is understood. You must learn to "say what you mean and mean what you say."

Our mind thinks at least six times faster than we can speak. Messages that are seen, heard, and understood by doing are the most likely to be retained.

Because the mind receives information so quickly, it often reacts even before the message is completed. Instead of viewing communication as information transmission (as many do), consider it more as idea transmission. That is, say or do something that will cause that idea to appear in your employee's head *and* ask the employee to speak back, restating the idea so you have conclusive proof it's in there! In this way you verify that she is involved. You have to think of a way to make the employee say it, for example, by asking questions. Therefore, you can improve communications with your employees by learning basic questioning skills.

An effective communicator learns to ask preparation questions. Before you ever talk to an employee, you must master the nine key preparation questions.

1. What background information exists?
2. What specific behaviors are at issue?
3. What are the consequences if things go unchanged?
4. What is the immediate objective?
5. What is my long-range goal?
6. What are the benefits of changed behavior?
7. How can this issue be described in the present tense?
8. How can I support this employee?
9. Am I in control and ready to discuss this situation?

It's also good to rehearse questions you can ask if an employee is shy, very quiet or resistant to your appraisal of her. Too often managers and supervisors find themselves talking too much during the appraisal and getting little or no employee feedback. Here are some ideas that can be used to draw out the quiet employee:

1. Inform the employee: "This position is important to our company and we feel we must make the best possible decision."

2. Ask the employee, "Does that make sense to you? Do you agree? What do you think we should do?"

3. Continue, "The more information we have, the better decisions we can make for our company and for you. Do you agree?"

4. State to the employee, "I feel it is important to talk directly with your peers. Do you have any problems with that?" (Watch closely for the reaction.)

5. Ask the employee, "When I talk with your co-workers, what will they tell me about . . . (start with easy questions)?"

6. Add a final comment, "I don't like surprises! Is there anything you would like to explain now before I talk with your former supervisors?"

7

THE PERFORMANCE APPRAISAL FACE-TO-FACE

Building Employee Participation

The questions we just looked at provide a good way to get into the heart of the interview and discuss the employee's self-analysis. In this section we'll look more closely at the techniques necessary to do so. Begin by realizing that you have already completed the hard part; you've begun the process by committing to deal with the employee, and you've set the time and place. Your objective now is to begin the interview so that you **maximize the employee's participation**. Let's look more closely at being face-to-face.

Make sure you do not begin a performance appraisal until you are in control of the issues and your emotions. Decide before the meeting the minimum action you will consider acceptable, what alternative solutions are available and when you expect performance to improve.

Set the stage by minimizing distractions and interruptions. Clear your desk and your mind of everything unrelated to the current situation. Hold the calls and close the door. Make sure you have read all the necessary paperwork and that it is at your disposal.

Make sure the temperature in the room is comfortable, water is available, and that the employee will be seated in a comfortable chair. Make the employee, not the appraisal form, the center of your focus. Make sure to allow enough time for the meeting so you don't have to end the discussion before it's completed.

You can make the person feel comfortable and welcome by beginning with a little casual conversation to get things started, but do not spend too much time on this. Sit face-to-face with no desk in between you if possible. This way, your body language will send the message that you're both on the same team, both trying to solve a common problem.

Structure the meeting by using a topical agenda, a brief order of events, so the employee knows what to expect. Begin by explaining why you are meeting and what is planned. Make sure the employee knows that every employee will participate in one of these meetings. It's part of your job and theirs. Also, make sure the employee understands that you will not be talking about money issues, that another meeting will be set up for that purpose. Instead, the focus is to talk about job performance and setting objectives for the future.

Explain that you are going to do the following:

- Find out how things are going in general.

- Ask the employee to explain how you can help make things better.

- Review the objectives of the job and the job description.

- Listen carefully to the employee's self-rating.

- Offer your own rating of the employee's strengths and weaknesses. Form a general impression of competence.

- Mutually agree on future goals for the employee.

Handling Employee Questions

Answer any questions the employee may have at any time during this explanation. Acknowledge the question and the feeling behind it. Let the employee know you understand. Respond directly to the concern. Get the employee's reaction. Make sure you've addressed the employee's concern before you move on.

Understand the types of questions employees have. Questions usually take the following shapes:

- *Hostile questions* such as, "Why do I have to be first?" or "Boy, are we going to talk about things you need to do, because there sure are a lot of them." These types of questions usually indicate the person is feeling threatened or angry about having to talk to you. Reflect the person's feeling by asking for more information until the employee has had a chance to vent his hostility, then move on to the heart of the interview.

- *Neutral questions* such as, "How long will this meeting take?" or "What do you mean by 'goals'?" These are clarifying questions. Your employee is unclear. Keep your responses simple. Answer as honestly and directly as you can and then move on.

- *Questions of concern* such as, "Will anyone else know what we talk about in this meeting?" or "Will all this go in my personnel record?" Your response needs to show you understand the employee's feeling. Again, answer as honestly and directly as you can before moving on.

HOW TO DO IT

Supervisor: Come in and sit down. Please relax. The purpose of this meeting is to evaluate your performance and for us to work out together the best path for your future. Have you brought the forms I asked you to fill out for today's meeting?

Employee: Yes. I have.

Supervisor: Excellent. I've filled out the same forms. I want to compare what we've written on these forms so we can see where we agree and disagree. You placed a great deal of emphasis on product changes, much more than I would.

Employee: Really? I enjoy that part of my job.

Supervisor: I really need your talents used in other areas. In fact, I'd like to see your time commitment changed by the next time we meet. Tell me, why do you think you spend so much time on product changes?

Employee: I think it's because the people in Department B are always coming to me with bits and pieces of things they want me to do or want me to change. Maybe we need better communication.

Supervisor: That's a good thought. I'll talk to the supervisor of Department B; maybe we can get something more productive worked out.

This scenario started with a comfortable opening and then set a direct path to discussing what was on the supervisor's mind. Some employees will need to spend more time on finding out how things are going, as we'll see below.

Finding out How Things Are Going

It's important to explore what's on the mind of your employee, thereby opening the door to mutual understanding. This sends a signal to your employee that you care about what he has to say, which is good for morale. It also clears the air for discussions to follow by giving the employee a chance to talk about his problems and concerns. This can be an early warning system! You gain perspective. By listening early, you build a give-and-take rapport with the employee that will be useful later. Remember, you are asking your employee to talk about his favorite topic . . . himself.

HOW TO DO IT

Supervisor: *(Leaning forward slightly)* How are things going for you here at ABC Company in general?

Employee: Well, I guess things are going pretty well for the most part . . . That's a little tough to answer all at once . . . I really don't know where to begin.

Supervisor: *(Nodding and smiling)* Yes, I understand. Take your time. I'm very interested in what you have to say.

Employee: Let's see. Things have been going pretty well. I like it here much more than my last job in Department B. I love my job. The atmosphere's a lot more relaxed and people seem to enjoy what they do.

Supervisor: *(Nodding)* Yes . . .

Employee: Well, I guess — oh! . . . the bonuses! Thank goodness for the bonuses! *(Smiling broadly)*

Supervisor: *(Smiling back)* Sounds as if you're pretty happy about the bonuses.

Employee: Am I ever! My daughter is in college, and boy, do those bonuses help!

Supervisor: Good, I'm glad you feel that way. Now, I'd like to hear about anything you don't like or any problems you've been having on the job.

Employee: Problems? *(Looking down and hesitating)* Ah . . . Well, for one thing, the work load gets fairly heavy sometimes, and I have a little trouble keeping up. All the managers act as if their work is the most important. They expect me to do everything "right now." And they get pretty upset if they don't get what they want right away.

Supervisor: I imagine that is difficult. *(Nodding)*

Employee: They have no knowledge of the work the other managers have already given me, and they don't seem to care about anything except their own work.

Supervisor: So you really feel major pressure at those times?

Employee: Sometimes I feel so tense I just want to run away. I don't know how to handle it. And then I start making mistakes. And that makes more work to correct, and I'm further behind!

Supervisor: I'm glad you told me about it. And I think there are a number of things we might do. *(Pause)* But let's talk about solutions to that problem a little later. I'd like to hear about any other problems you have before we get too deeply into solutions. I want to make sure I understand everything that is bothering you.

Employee: Okay. Well *(Pause)* There is . . . *(Pause)* it's uh *(Pause) (Much hesitation)* Susan . . . *(Pause)*

Supervisor: Susan?

Employee: I don't want to get anyone in trouble, but she can be very difficult at times.

Supervisor: When you say "difficult," how do you mean it?

Employee: It's related to the work load problem. We're supposed to help each other when the crunch is on. I'll ask her for some help and she'll say that she's busy, but then she seems to find the time to gab for a half-hour on the telephone while I'm breaking my neck to keep the managers off my back.

Supervisor: So you get pretty annoyed when she does that?

Employee: You bet! I guess I never realized how much I let it get to me; I've never said anything about it to her.

Supervisor: Okay, it sounds as if your main problems have to do with the work load, the pressure you feel from the managers, the mistakes that come from that situation, and Susan's unwillingness to help out when the crunch is on. Is that correct?

Employee: *(Nodding)* Right. And those really are big problems!

Supervisor: Yes, they are, and a little later we'll talk about some ways to deal with them. But now I'd like to move on to another subject. I'd like you to think about some ways I could make your job a little less frustrating and more satisfying for you. What ideas or suggestions do you have along those lines?

Employee: Let me see. Well, one thing is . . . I'd really like to know more about what everybody does around here.

Supervisor: So, you'd like to find out more about the nature of their jobs and how they fit into the big picture?

Employee: Yes.

Supervisor: What else can I do to make things less frustrating and more satisfying for you?

Employee: The computers in our department keep breaking down, and it always seems to be when we have deadlines.

Supervisor: Based on everything you've said so far, I need to work on three things to make life more satisfying and enjoyable for you around here. First, I need to speak to the managers about the work load problem. Maybe I can help them set up some kind of priority system so you don't get hit all at once with everything. Second, I may have to speak with Susan about being more cooperative when the crunch is on.

Employee: *(Nervously)* Are you sure that's a good idea? Will she know we talked? I don't want her thinking I'm a rat.

Supervisor: I can appreciate that. But, believe me, I won't handle it that way. As I said when I asked you to meet with me, I'll be doing this sort of thing with everybody.

Employee: Okay.

Supervisor: Third, I think it would be a good idea if I arranged for you to meet some of the other people in the department so you could understand the roles they play.

Employee: I'd like that.

Supervisor: Great! And then fourth, I need to have the computers looked at. Okay, I'd like to move on to another topic, your work performance.

Before you begin your performance appraisal, recognize that discussing employee performance is where you are most likely to encounter initial resistance. Identifying problem behavior patterns helps set the stage for effective action.

One of the major types of problem behaviors is hostility. Hostile people bully or even overwhelm others; usually, they make critical remarks. Give the hostile employee time to run down. Don't answer shouting with shouting. Get him to sit down and keep eye contact. State your own opinions firmly and don't act frightened. Stand up to him without fighting. If the shouting continues, ask the employee to leave and come back when he has calmed down.

HOW TO DO IT

Employee: *(Agitated)* I tell you, some changes better get made at this company soon, or a lot of people are going to quit. And I'm not the only one who'll tell you that!

Supervisor: I hear a lot of anger in your voice. *(Leaning forward slightly)* I'd like to hear how you're feeling.

Employee: *(Slightly startled)* Well, I am really angry! I don't know whose fault it is, but we don't get much management. We're left on our own to make key decisions, and then we're criticized for making the wrong ones! Everyone around here thinks the quality of management in this company leaves much to be desired!

Supervisor: *(Looking directly into the employee's eyes)* Sounds as if your anger has a lot to do with the direct supervision you're getting . . . or maybe that you're not getting. Isn't that anger really directed at me?

Employee: *(A little flustered)* I . . . didn't mean anything about you personally. Well . . . uh, that's not true either. It does have something to do with you.

Supervisor: I really want to hear what's on your mind, even if it is critical of me. Level with me and be as direct as you can. *(Puts down pen and faces employee, giving full attention)* What suggestions do you have for how I could improve the way I supervise?

Employee: Sometimes you give me a lot of work to do without telling me why I should do it. I waste a lot of my time doing things for no purpose at all. It makes me feel like I'm not important enough for you to take the time to make sure I understand. And usually there is no priority assigned to the work, so I'm never sure where I should start.

Supervisor: So one thing I could do is explain the purpose of the work I assign to you, giving a better idea of why I want it done, why it's important and what priority it has?

Employee: That would help a lot. A whole lot. And there are some other things . . . if you're sure you'd like to hear them. *(Smiling)*

Supervisor: *(Smiling)* I would like to hear them. Go ahead . . .

Often critical remarks are rooted in anger, resulting in hostility. In this scenario, you can see how the supervisor allowed the employee to vent his feelings and afterwards directed the conversation productively. Let's continue to learn from this exchange.

HOW TO DO IT

Supervisor: You've been very honest with me, so I think I've got a pretty good idea about some of your problems. I'd like to wait to talk about solutions until a little later . . .

Employee: *(Interrupting)* What do you mean "wait to talk about solutions" until later? What's the sense of identifying problems if you don't want to talk about them? I just told you how upset I am and now you don't want to talk about how to solve the problems?

Supervisor: You're angry and irritated that I changed the subject before talking about solutions, is that right? *(Reflecting feeling)*

Employee: Yeah! I mean, it just doesn't make any sense. This whole thing is beginning to feel like a total waste of time.

Supervisor: You're saying that you want to talk about solutions right now, not after we've discussed anything else.

Employee: That's exactly what I'm saying, and I mean it!

Supervisor: I also think talking about solutions to the problems you mentioned is very important. I plan to spend a lot of time later in this interview to do just that, but I wanted to talk about some other things first. I'd like to hear your suggestions for how I could make your job more satisfying, and we need to do a thorough review of your work performance.

Employee: Well, I think it's more important to talk about solutions while the problems are still fresh in our minds.

Supervisor: Let's step back from this for just a minute to get a fresh perspective. It seems we disagree on how to proceed. You'd like to discuss solutions to some of the problems you identified right now. You feel it's important and you want to get it solved. I do too, but I'd like to talk about solutions after we've covered some other areas so I have a good understanding of the total picture. I'd like to find a way out of this disagreement, preferably with a solution that we both can live with so we can get on with improving things for both of us. What do you think is our next step?

> **Employee**: *(Pauses while thinking)* I don't really know.
> *(Smiling)* We can always do it my way . . . *(Laughing)*
> Well, we can maybe spend a few minutes talking about
> solutions to the things I told you were big problems to
> me. Then, if it looks as if we're not going to come up
> with any real solutions very quickly, or if we have more
> to talk about, we can talk about it again later in the
> interview.
>
> **Supervisor**: Very good idea. Suppose we spend fifteen
> minutes now talking about some potential solutions?

You can see how the emotion was controlled while a compromise evolved. The employee in this situation felt he was being heard and was playing an active role in the interview. This sort of feeling lays the groundwork for true communication.

Problem Behavior and What to Do in a Performance Appraisal

There are other types of behavior problems besides hostility.

Complainers are people who gripe incessantly but never do anything about their problems. With these people,

1. Listen.
2. Acknowledge their feelings. Feelings are always valid.
3. Paraphrase the facts.
4. Move to problem-solving.

Unresponsive people respond only with yes/no answers or silence. Ask open-ended questions and wait patiently. Lean slightly toward the employee using body language to show your interest, and inform the employee of what he must do to put the problem behind him.

Too agreeable people, while being very supportive, rarely produce what they say they will, or they act contrary to the way you have been led to expect. Bring to the surface the underlying facts and ask for their feedback, especially negative. Be prepared to move toward action, expectations and deadlines.

Negative people always respond with comments like, "It won't work." Your task is to present often optimistic but realistic statements about past successes while making sure the problem is thoroughly discussed both positively and negatively. Highly analytical people need sufficient time before you can expect them to act positively, avoiding negative tendencies.

Know-it-alls appear as condescending, pompous, imposing people who sometimes really are experts. Make sure you prepare yourself well before meeting with the "know-it-all." Structure your questions toward facts and then raise problems. Ask "what-if" questions to assist in re-examining your concerns.

Stallers slow down their decision-making until others make a decision for them. They have trouble letting go of anything until everything is perfect, which it never is. You must make it easy for stallers to tell you about conflicts or reservations that prevent their decisions. Listen for indirect clues that may provide insight into problem areas and give support after a decision is made. Try to keep any action steps as your responsibility.

Criers have problems controlling their emotions, and the tears show it. Often they are as embarrassed and as uncomfortable as you are. You can leave the room and let the employee gain composure, but identify the discomfort both of you are feeling as you leave.

Any of these behaviors can cause difficulty during a performance appraisal. When an employee refuses to go along with the game plan, you can use the STOP-LOOK-LISTEN APPROACH.

STOP-LOOK-LISTEN APPROACH

Stop the interaction before it becomes argumentative or unproductive.

Don't get angry.

Don't get defensive.

Don't blame others.

Don't lecture.

Look squarely at the problem and describe it succinctly to the employee.

Listen for suggestions and ways to resolve the problem together.

Another problem can arise when an employee talks too much. When this happens, decrease the use of verbal and nonverbal encouragement. That is, don't smile and nod as much. You can also cut down on direct eye contact.

Close the subject. Move to a new topic by setting time limits and reminding the employee of all that must be discussed. Reward concise answers with positive feedback.

Asking Your Employee How You Can Help

You may think you don't want to ask how you can help because:

- It's threatening.
- You expect the worst.
- You think the employee should ask the question, not you.

You *should* ask this question because:

- Employees love it.
- It gives you feedback on how you're doing as a boss.
- You'll begin to hear common themes.
- You'll gain perspective.
- It may unlock the door to increased performance.
- It lays the groundwork for creating performance agreement.

One of your objectives during the performance appraisal is to use your experience by adding to the alternatives your employee has to select from when faced with making a decision. Your employee may not see what you see, so help him.

Setting the Course for Action

Now comes the actual work of unifying all the elements into a constructive outcome by appraising performance and communicating the appraisal successfully to your employee.

The performance appraisal is a summary of your work observations. After each key area of accountability in your employee's job description is evaluated, his overall performance is evaluated. The results are summarized on the next page.

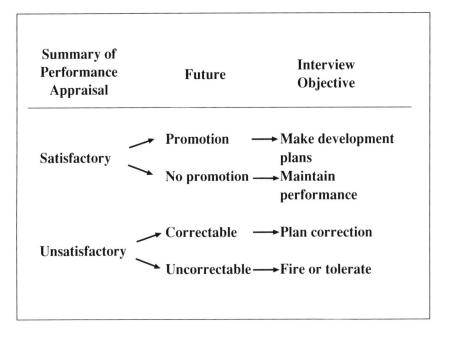

Summary of Performance Appraisal	Future	Interview Objective
Satisfactory	Promotion	Make development plans
	No promotion	Maintain performance
Unsatisfactory	Correctable	Plan correction
	Uncorrectable	Fire or tolerate

Let's look at each one of these areas by beginning with unsatisfactory performance. There are two types — correctable and uncorrectable. The most important question to ask yourself in contemplating how to correct unsatisfactory performance is "What is *influencing* poor performance?"

Consult your performance log. If you built your log correctly, after you observed a performance discrepancy, you should have *collected valid information* on your employee's performance and included it in the log from the onset. This eliminates surprises later. Your analysis of nonperformance should reveal trends. If there are no trends, you may have observed a simple blip that's minimally worth pursuing; but if there are trends, the formal, sit-down performance appraisal session is the place to address performance concerns.

You must be extremely careful when determining the reasons for nonperformance. What originally got your attention was a *symptom of nonperformance*, not the cause. You must make sure the employee knows precisely what he is to do so that his behavior can change. For you to effectively monitor and help the employee change, you must know precisely what the behavior or the problem is. Your performance log will help you with this. It will also help answer the question "Does the employee know that his performance is not what it should be?" Direct, specific questions should be asked on a day-to-day basis to clarify your log entries. Here are two questions you should learn to ask:

> "Do you know what your error rate is?"

> "Do you know how many days you arrived late for work in the last two weeks?"

Also look at your internal support systems. Feedback should not always have to pass through you to get to the employee. One of today's management goals is empowered workers!

This is a listing of common reasons why employees don't do what they're supposed to do. Use these potential reasons to organize yourself.

What's causing the problem?

_____   Not knowing what he is supposed to do.

_____   Not knowing how to do it.

_____   Not knowing why he should do it.

_____   Fear of future negative consequences.

_____   Experiencing personal problems.

_____   Not recognizing personal limits.

_____   Perceiving obstacles beyond his control.

_____   Thinking your way will not work.

_____   Thinking his way is better.

_____   Thinking something else is more important.

_____   Assuming no one could do it.

_____   Thinking he is already doing it.

_____   Being rewarded for not doing it.

_____   Receiving no negative consequence for performing poorly.

Remember, your employees must know exactly what you want in order to supply it, and must know exactly what the consequences are if they don't. That's where your careful analysis of each employee's job description and your discussion of job duties, expectations and consequences come in to play. We will discuss preparation shortly.

Ask yourself if your objectives in this performance appraisal should be limited. Is there a limit to how much criticism your employee can absorb in one session? It may be too much to expect performance improvements in multiple areas within six months or even one year. However, you should know what improvements can be made and then gain the commitment from the employee to make them.

If you must select limited objectives, ask yourself the following questions:

- Which deficiencies are most critical to the company?

- Does the employee possess the confidence necessary to make the multiple changes?

- Can improvements be continuous, i.e., spread out over the calendar year rather than tackled all at once?

Plan how you are going to help the employee accept the need to improve. Compliance does not necessarily mean acceptance, and the best results come from acceptance, from the employee stating that improvement is needed.

How much improvement is enough?

- Get the employee to commit to a specific plan for improvement.

- Distinguish between *improvement* and *correction*. Correction is the overall goal. Improvement is progress in the right direction.

If the performance remains unsatisfactory or is not correctable, or if the person lacks the capacity or the desire to improve, you have some options. You can continue to tolerate the unsatisfactory performance or begin a termination interview, no longer focusing on appraisal. Consult with the personnel department or your boss for information on how to proceed. Remember, once you decide an employee's nonperformance is occurring because of some unchangeable limitation, you have closed the door to other alternatives. You are no longer managing that employee, and you can only watch what happens.

Now, let's look at the employee who has satisfactory performance but has no chance of promotion. There are two types of people here . . . those who already know and accept the low probability of promotion and those who either don't know it or don't accept it. Every organization has people who should be promoted but won't be. These people are sometimes referred to as having "plateaued."

Those who don't accept their low probability of promotion will either rise, possibly in another company, or they will cause you problems.

Good performance does not, for many reasons, always ensure promotion. For employees for whom there is no promotion ahead, you must define the employee's objectives clearly. Focus on these issues:

- What will sustain this employee's current performance? This type of employee will have a large need for positive reinforcement.

- What will motivate this employee? This question must be answered in terms of the person's immediate unmet needs.

- What specific motivators would be effective with this employee? Delegate often to him, transferring your authority where possible.

- How can you provide job enrichment, stretching his job to offer greater challenges? Different from delegation, such changes are permanent, and can come from others' work as well as your own.

- Is it possible to encourage participation, giving a larger share in decision-making?

- Is this employee capable of being involved in mentoring other employees? Recognize that transferring knowledge is an important contribution to the success of the company.

Some employees don't realize there is no promotion ahead for them. They need to know their position clearly.

1. Hold the conversation in a favorable appraisal setting. Be supportive, explaining the outcome gently, and then look for ways to truly discuss the job at hand.

2. Try to identify possible blockages while admitting that you don't have all the answers or control the promotion process.

By comparison, the interview for employees whose performance is satisfactory and for whom promotion lies ahead becomes a development interview, although promotion should not be guaranteed.

Your objective here is to shift the emphasis from present performance to preparation for a future job. Stress that development for the employee's next job does not overshadow the need to maintain satisfactory performance on his current job, but that the new duties will supplement it. Verify realistic employee career plans and together build the plan for the future.

Possible development actions include:

• On-the-job development

• Personal coaching

• Planned exposure to new positions or duties

• In-house or off-the-job development

• Workshops, seminars, conferences

• Self-development and self-study

• College courses and advanced degrees

You can consult the following general performance guidelines when you talk to your employee, whether the employee is performing satisfactorily or not, is promotable or not:

- Use your log and appraisal form as a guide only.

- Start with the positive.

- Establish as much agreement as you can between your analysis and the employee's analysis.

- Be ready to shift from talking to listening.

- Get your employee's reaction to your analysis.

- Give direction after the employee reacts to your appraisal.

- Don't promise anything you can't deliver.

HOW TO DO IT

Supervisor: *(Nodding and then pausing for several seconds before speaking)* Anything else you want to add?

Employee: I really think that pretty much covers all the areas I wanted to talk about today.

Supervisor: Good. You provided me with a very complete and thoughtful analysis of your job performance and how things are going for you. You really seemed to get into it!

Employee: *(Smiling and obviously pleased)* Yes, I did.

Supervisor: Now, as I mentioned a little earlier, I'd like to add a few things to what you've said.

Employee: This is the part I've been dreading . . .

Supervisor: You're a little concerned about what I have to say about your performance?

Employee: Yes . . . as well as this seems to be going, I guess I am a little apprehensive. It isn't always the easiest thing to have somebody give you honest and objective feedback on how you're doing on your job. You're afraid to hear some things. You know they are probably true, but it's hard to face them. Especially, when it comes from your boss.

Supervisor: *(Nodding and smiling but saying nothing)*

Employee: That's all I was thinking . . . I guess I'm ready to listen . . . *(Leaning forward slightly)*

Supervisor: *(Smiling)* I asked you to start with the areas where you think you're performing well. I'd like to do the same thing.

Employee: *(Smiling)* Good . . . I don't mind starting there!

Supervisor: One of the areas where you felt you were performing effectively was in making presentations. I'm in full agreement with that. Three of our most demanding managers have told me that you make excellent presentations, and they don't hand out compliments easily.

Employee: *(Smiling and looking a little embarrassed)* That's nice to know.

Supervisor: Yes, it is nice. Another thing, our training department has asked if they could use you as an instructor for new employee training.

Employee: *(A little surprised)* No, I didn't know that. I am really interested in being able to do that . . .

Supervisor: I'm glad. Let's talk about that in more detail later.

Employee: I'm looking forward to it!

Supervisor: Another area that you mentioned you were doing pretty well in is following up on leads the sales people give you. Again, I'm in full agreement.

Employee: *(Nodding)*

Supervisor: At least three of our customers have told me they would never have considered, much less chosen, our line if it hadn't been for your persistent following up. That's exactly what we want our inside sales people to do.

Employee: *(Smiling)* I hope they weren't saying I was bugging them too much.

Supervisor: Now I'd like to talk about some areas that you didn't mention where I think you're performing effectively.

Employee: *(Smiling and leaning forward a little)* Okay, that won't be hard to listen to . . .

Supervisor: A lot of the things you do around here have a motivating, almost inspirational, effect on others. Ever since we've been working together, I've noticed you're always trying to help the people here.

Employee: *(Smiling and nodding)* Yes, well, I would want someone to do that for me. I just do what's right.

Supervisor: *(Smiling and nodding)* I think "helpful" is a good way to characterize what you do. Let's talk about another area where I think you're performing effectively on the job. In fact, it's an area in which I think you could stand to improve. *(Pause)* I'd like to explain my thinking and get your reactions. And finally, I'd like us to reach some agreement on what you could work on to improve your performance over the next couple of months. *(Pause)*

Employee: Okay.

Supervisor: And after that, I'd like us to agree on what I'm going to do to help you improve in these areas.

Employee: Sounds good.

Supervisor: One area where I think you could improve is in handling objections.

Employee: *(Wrinkling forehead)* Handling objections? I disagree. I think I'm good at handling objections. In fact, I even keep a notebook on objections so I can come up with better and better arguments. I practice delivering responses to objections so I can deliver them with confidence.

Supervisor: When a prospect offers an objection, such as it's too expensive or it's not compatible without other equipment, it's awfully tempting to come back with an argument to overcome the objection.

Employee: *(Nodding)* Absolutely.

Supervisor: But often the best thing to do is to get more information, draw the guy out. You want to get him talking.

Employee: If I drew him out, I would know more about what's bothering him and what he really thinks is important, what he really wants.

Supervisor: It seems you're willing to consider that as a possible strategy for handling objections? I admire that about you. You are always looking for ways to improve. Why don't we move on to another area? A second area I'd like to see some improvement in is meeting deadlines.

Employee: *(Shaking his head and smiling)* I knew those reports were going to creep into this conversation. I hate those reports, and you know it. They're a big waste of time. I'd rather be selling.

Supervisor: Sounds as if you find the reports unpleasant, almost as though they are an obstacle to getting more important things done? *(Reflecting feeling)*

Employee: *(Sighing)* Yes, that's just how I feel. I wish we could automate the process so the data would just be there as we made our calls.

Supervisor: I'm not big on paperwork either. On the other hand, if those reports don't get in on time, it causes lots of problems. Until we computerize the department, we're just going to have to do those reports. *(Pause)* Maybe at this point it would be helpful if you reviewed for both of us the specific ways your reports can get done. OK?

Finalizing Performance Improvement Plans

At this point in the review, you will identify:

- Specific tasks the employee is going to work on within a defined time frame.

- Specific tasks you are going to work on during the same time frame to help the employee improve performance, removing frustrations and roadblocks.

The next step is to develop a written record designed to help both of you keep the agreement. It contains these items:

- Specific tasks the employee can work on to improve his performance.

- Specific tasks for you to work on that will assist and support your employee.

- Specific tasks that will make the employee's job less frustrating and more satisfying while building for the future.

The list of specific tasks you compile needs to be prioritized. It should contain short- and long-term objectives. Develop a plan of action that can be broken down into meaningful and achievable steps.

Use the following strategy:

- Ask what the employee would like to work on.

- Make additional suggestions on what you would like the employee to work on.

- Reach agreement on exactly what the employee will do first.

- Ask what you can do to help.

- Make additional suggestions, if necessary, on things you can accomplish.

- Reach agreement on exactly what will be done by you and when it will be done.

- Write it down.

HOW TO DO IT

Supervisor: Why don't you take a few minutes to talk about the specific things that you'd like to be working on over the next several weeks, given all the things that we've talked about so far?

Employee: Maybe I ought to put the worst first. Once I get that under control, the rest will be much easier. I'll make a commitment to get those monthly reports in on time every month for . . .

Supervisor: Say the next three months?

Employee: That sounds reasonable.

Supervisor: Great. What else? *(Beginning to make some notes)*

Employee: Well . . . I would like to work on learning new products.

Supervisor: *(Nodding and making more notes)* We've got getting your monthly reports in on time for the next three months and working on new products.

Employee: I still would like to do a better job of getting interviews with prospects. But I'll need some help in critiquing how I'm doing it now. Perhaps if we could spend some time role playing, I could get better at it.

Supervisor: *(Nodding)* Okay. Sounds good. Anything else?

Employee: I think that about covers it. I can't think of anything else.

Supervisor: *(Glancing at his notes)* You mentioned getting all your monthly reports in on time for the next three months, learning new products, and doing a better job of getting interviews. Does that pretty much cover it?

Employee: Yes.

Supervisor: Before we actually write down the tasks, I'd like to add a couple of ideas. Then we'll pare down the list to a manageable size.

The interview would proceed with the supervisor and employee listing all the areas needing work, setting reasonable dates for things to be done, and discussing all the ways the supervisor can help the employee achieve the objective.

Closing the Performance Appraisal Interview

In closing the review, ask for your employee's reaction.

- If an employee seems angry, agitated or upset, devote time to talking about these feelings.

- Help the employee come up with a solution to the problem.

- If you have different ideas on how to proceed, use the stop-look-listen approach outlined earlier.

Share your reaction to the performance interview with your employee. If you are pleased, share your positive feelings. If you are not pleased, be honest without being brutal. Don't put the blame for what happened entirely on the employee. Try to stress the positive. Describe the specific problems briefly and objectively. Ask for suggestions on how the problem can be solved or avoided in future meetings, trying to reach a win-win status.

Schedule the follow-up meeting, and end on a positive note. Walk the employee out in a friendly manner. Thank the employee and tell him you are looking forward to the follow-up meeting.

8

IMPROVING PERFORMANCE APPRAISAL INTERVIEWING SKILLS

Skill Building

Appraisal and interviewing is a science. You can acquire the skills that can help you relate constructively and communicate more successfully with every employee. Study the following prime areas. Each affects your ability to concentrate, and each causes the employee to believe you care.

You must be aware of your *attending behavior*. This refers to your general behavior while you are interacting with the employee. Let's look at the basic components of healthy behavior.

1. Make eye contact. Look the employee in the eye when talking **AND** listening.

2. Use good body language. Aim your body at the listener; lean forward slightly. Use your facial muscles actively, but naturally. Don't be a stone face, and don't forget to smile occasionally!

3. Use gestures to support your facial message. Minimize distracting mannerisms, overused phrases or clichés. Don't reuse the same example, and don't let distracting mannerisms get in your way so that the employee pays more attention to your mannerisms than your message. Practice your delivery in front of a mirror or videotape a mock interview. Study the videotape carefully in order to improve your communication ability.

4. Vary your speaking style to improve the chances that your message is heard and understood. When you are serious, make your points slowly and with emphasis. When you are enthusiastic, speed up and raise your pitch.

5. Become skilled at asking questions and gathering information. Invite your employee to talk. **Be prepared to stop talking and start listening at any time**. You are not on stage or carrying out a monologue here. This is not a lecture but a guided conversation.

6. As you become involved in discussion, focus attention on a specific topic, but give the employee latitude to respond. Get rid of the feeling of interrogation.

7. Watch for clues. Continuing to talk when you know a person is not listening is a waste of time. If the employee exhibits any of the following behaviors, it means she is not listening:

   • Holding out her hand as if to say "Stop."

   • Looking confused.

- Rolling her eyes toward the ceiling.

- Beginning to interrupt.

- Constantly looking away.

What's the best way to avoid sounding like an interrogator? When questioning employees, the general rule is that it is better to be descriptive than judgmental, to be supportive rather than authoritarian, and to set a tone of equality, not superiority.

By being descriptive, not judgmental, you show the employee that you are interested in solving a problem, not in finding a scapegoat, someone to blame.

- *Judgmental:* "How could you do such a stupid thing?"

- *Descriptive:* "Can you explain what caused the problem?"

By being supportive, not authoritarian, you help eliminate resentfulness and defensiveness. It is better to show an attitude of respect for the employee's ability to problem-solve.

- *Authoritarian:* "This is what you do to solve this problem."

- *Supportive:* "What do you think we should do to solve this problem, and how can I help?"

If you put too much emphasis on your position and power, you may create a barrier between you and your employee. However, if you seek employee opinions and share information, a feeling of equality is created.

- *Superiority:* "I used to do your job, and this is the way it's done."

- *Equality:* "This is the way this has been done in the past, but I would like to hear how you think it could be done better."

Remember, you learn more from listening than from talking. The first highly effective listening technique is *reflecting* or summarizing. This technique captures the gist of what the other person says, putting it in your words. It helps prevent misunderstanding and stimulates your thinking.

Reflecting an employee's feelings is a simple, two-part process:

- You identify the feeling behind the other person's remark: confusion, anger, frustration, excitement, determination, etc.

- You reflect the feeling back to the employee, beginning your response with words such as: "You're feeling . . ." or "Sounds as if you're feeling . . ."

When you respond to, reflect or summarize an employee's feelings in this way, you send an important message: "I'm as interested in your feelings as I am in your thoughts and ideas."

Another fundamental communication technique is to speak in specific terms. Here are six ways to build effective communication skills during your appraisals:

1. Focus on closing; speaking "fuzzily" is distracting and unproductive.

   - Fuzzy: "Work on your attitude."

   - Specific: "I need more work from you when my reports are due. OK?" Ask for more work.

2. Focus on the facts. Avoid emotionally loaded expressions or criticisms that include insulting words, e.g., "That was stupid."

3. Watch out for exaggeration, e.g., "That was the most ridiculous thing anyone could have said." Be specific and accurate in your comments.

HOW NOT TO DO IT

"You have a bad temper. Stop throwing temper tantrums."

HOW TO DO IT

"You need to work on staying calm. Let's talk about some specific ways to do that."

4. Watch your pacing and timing. Pause after your main points, giving them a chance to sink in. Make sure the employee stays with you. Tell her what you're going to tell her; tell her; then tell her what you told her.

5. Strive for rapport. Reflecting feeling captures the emotions. Reflecting does not mean you agree with a statement. Using this technique, your task is only to mirror the employee's statement.

6. Summarize frequently. Summarizing focuses the main points.

Here are some points to remember:

- You do not make change happen by lecturing.

- We have little ability to get people to do things they do not want to do.

- The way people function is somehow part of them; they do not change easily.

- Resistance is softened when people feel they can discuss their opinions and be heard.

During the appraisal session, **you should do only 10% of the talking**. You are the catalyst of change, getting employees to do most of the talking. Most supervisors tend to dominate conversations. How do you change this?

- Learn to be quiet and understand the value of silence. Silence rarely offends. It is normally nonjudgmental if accompanied by the correct, open, attending behavior. The raised eyebrow with the expectant look, uncrossed arms and legs, and facing the employee directly are all examples of nonjudgmental silence that encourages your employee to talk.

- Know how to use questions effectively. You must become skilled in the use of the different types of questions. Be conscious of the kind of responses a question will generate before asking it. **It is the *form* of the question that determines the extent of the response.**

Restrictive or *closed-ended* questions prevent thought-provoking answers and discourage productive discussion. Examples are: How long? When did you . . . ? Who wrote this?

Primarily, three types of questions work in getting employees to talk. Use these as alternatives to restrictive or closed questions:

- Open-Ended Questions
- Reflective Questions
- Directive Questions

1. *Open-Ended Questions*

   Open-ended questions get at attitudes, feelings, opinions and other useful information about the person. Examples include: How do you feel about . . . What could we do to . . . Why has this . . . ?

Open-ended questions can be successfully combined with the hypothetical problem. Examples include: Suppose you were . . . How would you do it if you were . . . What action would you take if . . . ?

Open-ended questions can also be combined with commands. For example: Tell me more . . . Give me more detail . . . Keep talking . . .

HOW TO DO IT

Employee: "Our results would improve if we modified the method we used to manufacture that part."

Supervisor: "You're convinced the results can be improved?"

---

2. *Reflective Questions*

Reflective questions can help you avoid arguments, because you are responding without accepting or rejecting what the employee said. It shows that you understand, that you were listening, and that you heard what the employee said. This also implies that you understand how she feels. Reflective questions encourage employees to expand on what they have said, leading to deeper levels of communication and understanding. If an employee has said something illogical or untrue, hearing it repeated helps her see the problems in it.

HOW TO DO IT

"It sounds like something is really bothering you. Is there anything else you'd like to say?"

---

3. *Directive Questions*

Directive questions obtain specific information. Such questions are usually used after the other types of questions have been tried and communication between you and your employee is strong.

HOW TO DO IT

"If you're convinced the results can be improved, exactly what would you do and when would you do it?"

Combining different types of questions in your interview will stimulate the employee to participate. Pick the tools that are best for the job.

Once you get the employee talking, how do you respond to keep the conversation going? Use responses that focus and encourage, or the conversation will go off track or stop. Refrain from one-upmanship. Your objective is to stimulate the employee to suggest ideas. If you argue the merits of ideas as the employee says them, you waste idea-giving time. If you reject ideas as they are given, you may punish idea-giving behavior and discourage further discussion. If you reinforce good ideas when they come up before all ideas are out, it's easy for the employee to stop searching. A productive appraisal depends on the interaction of ideas. Some of the best ideas come from bad ideas, so stimulate the process and get *all* the ideas on the table.

HOW TO DO IT

Supervisor: Please tell me any problems you've been having.

Employee: The new computers are down more than they're up. Is somebody going to do something about that? I can't get my work done on time.

Supervisor: Sounds as if you're pretty angry about that.

Employee: I am!

Interviewing Attitudes

1. Avoid being defensive yourself — the person with tact gets things done without hostility.

2. Think positively about where you're trying to go rather than being negative about where you are now.

3. Think about growth, development, progress and accomplishment.

4. Don't use words that point to negative behavior. You are not trying to excuse the past; you're planning for a better future.

5. Don't use *never, ever, always, every time, invariably, without exception,* etc. These terms trigger negative responses. Avoid profanity. Your language should be tactful but firm.

6. Control the interview. Your control is essential to a productive interview and to getting the employee's commitment to plan an improvement.

7. Focus the interview so you and the employee have to work on solutions. Discuss possible ways to improve, and decide how to begin.

8. Decide together what help the employee needs. Decide what you need to do to accomplish high-priority tasks. Be specific.

   • State the nature of the improvement sought.

   • State the quantity of the improvement sought.

   • Define dates when progress is to be checked.

   • Agree on who is going to do what.

Stay the course and communicate your message. Remember, the formal, sit-down performance appraisal interview is conversation that gets somewhere. It has objectives, an orderly track and results in concrete agreements. It is conversational, but the employee does most of the talking.

Another frequently overlooked but highly effective skill you should perfect is body language. Body language sometimes communicates more about a person's real feelings than the person can. The more skilled you become at watching body language and picking up on these signals, the more effective you will become during performance appraising. In the important and sensitive business of performance appraisals, it isn't an option, it's a necessity.

Equality can be expressed in everything, from the initial handshake to the image left at the close of the interview. It is important not to stand or tower over your employee during the performance appraisal, starting from the time you ask your employee to meet with you.

The next most important thing to watch is eye contact. Avoiding eye contact can indicate disagreement, an unwillingness to continue to talk or dishonesty. Confident people have more eye contact than those who are unsure or attempting to conceal, and the duration of their contact is longer. Confident people blink less, hence they also seem to be better listeners.

Gestures are almost as important as eye contact. One of the key gestures is crossing the arms across the chest as if to protect yourself against the individual, sometimes indicating you'd rather not move. Different from a comfortable position, this gesture usually involves gripping the arms or clenched fists.

Your response should be to draw out the feelings of subordinates who have crossed their arms and find out what their needs are. Reconsider what you are doing or saying to employees who have crossed their arms, because they are signalling strongly that they have withdrawn from the conversation. Getting agreement on anything, even on entirely unrelated topics, becomes more difficult after the arms are crossed and a person has become defensive. Failing to recognize the early signs of discontent or disagreement results in painful and unproductive communications.

Another key body language signal to watch out for is posture. Slouching can indicate indifference. Does the employee look interested? If not, find out why. A confident and open person will talk without covering her mouth and will stand and sit straight in an open posture.

In a study of negotiating techniques, it was found that the atmosphere for reaching settlements was enhanced when negotiators uncrossed their legs and moved toward each other.

Crossing of legs and leaning away are parts of a family of behaviors that communicate suspicion, uncertainty, rejection, or doubt. Other examples of such behaviors include physically moving the body away from the person, having the feet or entire body pointing to the exit, sending a sideways glance, taking a sideways position and squirming in the chair.

Watch your employee's body language for important clues. Even more important, evaluate your own body language so that it:

1. Sends positive messages about your openness, understanding, and willingness to listen to the employee.

2. Does not send messages of superiority, defensiveness, or closed-mindedness.

9

FOLLOW-UP

Lack of follow-up is one of the most common supervisory failures. Informal follow-ups begin immediately after the appraisal interview. Follow up immediately and touch base frequently.

Ask your employee to follow up with you. Be sure he knows you meant what you said about working together by staying on top of what you agreed to work on together. Answer any questions immediately. These actions solidify the two-way relationship between you and your employee and make certain that the spotlight isn't totally on the employee.

Reinforce changed behavior immediately! It is better to praise positive behavior than to criticize negative behavior. Do this as behavior occurs; don't wait for the next formal meeting. Changing behavior is hard work. Periodic encouragement from you is necessary to prevent the employee from returning to the inappropriate behavior. The most critical aspect of follow-up is *timeliness*.

The structure of the follow-up interview is similar to that of the original performance appraisal interview. Analyze both your employee's and your own performance.

- Have the goals been accomplished?

- In what specific ways have the goals been exceeded or missed?

- Why weren't the goals accomplished?

- What needs to be done to get them accomplished?

Review progress, ask the employee's opinion and give your own. Verify agreement on all main points before proceeding to the negative issues.

Decide where you want to go. For example, if major progress has been made, you can afford to schedule the next formal follow-up meeting farther into the future. If little progress has been made but a lot of effort has been expended, you can renegotiate the agreement, adjusting the "when" aspect. You may revise your goals, taking smaller steps. If, on the other hand, little progress has been made and little effort has been expended, this may signal that a termination is in order. Ask the employee for solutions. Ask the employee to think about the consequences of nonperformance, i.e., demotion, termination, etc.

Your next step is to close the interview. Get the employee's overall reaction to how things went. Give your own thoughts and feelings as well. Schedule your next follow-up meeting to make sure you and your employee accomplish your goals! End the interview on a positive note.

10

FORMS, PRACTICES AND CHECKSHEETS

PERFORMANCE APPRAISAL CHECKLIST

PREPARATION

_____ I have reviewed mutually understood expectations with respect to job duties, projects, goals, standards, and any performance factors pertinent to this appraisal discussion.

_____ I have measured job performance against mutually understood expectations. I have done my best to avoid such pitfalls as:

- Allowing bias/prejudice to be a factor.
- Not consulting my performance log and relying on my memory alone.
- Overly focusing on some aspects of the job at the expense of others.
- Being overly influenced by my own experience.
- Using trait evaluation rather than performance measurement.

_____ I have reviewed the employee's background including:

- Skills
- Work experience
- Training
- Past performance
- Attendance records

_____ I have identified the employee's performance strengths and determined areas in need of improvement. In so doing, I have:

- Accumulated specific documentation to communicate my position.
- Limited myself to those critical points that are the most important.
- Prepared a development plan in case the employee needs assistance in coming up with a suitable plan.
- Identified areas for concentration for the next appraisal period.
- Given the employee advance notice of when the discussion will be held so that he/she can prepare.
- Set aside an adequate block of uninterrupted time to permit a full and complete discussion.

CONDUCTING THE APPRAISAL DISCUSSION

_____ I plan to begin the discussion by creating a sincere, open and friendly atmosphere. This includes:
- Reviewing the purpose of the discussion.
- Making it clear that it is a joint discussion for the purpose of mutual problem-solving and goal-setting.
- Striving to put the employee at ease.

_____ In the body of the discussion, I intend to keep the focus on job performance and related factors. This includes:
- Discussing job requirements, employee strengths and accomplishments, improvements needed; evaluating results of performance against objectives set during previous reviews and discussions.
- Being prepared to cite observations for each point I want to discuss.
- Encouraging the employee to appraise his/her own performance.
- Using open, reflective and directive questions to promote thought.

_____ I will encourage the employee to outline his/her personal plans for self-development before suggesting ideas of my own. In the process, I will:
- Get the employee to set growth and improvement targets.
- Reach agreement on appropriate development plans, set a timetable and explain the support I am prepared to give.
- Be prepared to discuss work assignments, projects and goals for the next appraisal period, asking the employee to prepare suggestions.

CLOSING THE DISCUSSION

_____ I will be prepared to make notes during the discussion for the purpose of summarizing agreements and follow-up. In closing, I will
- Summarize what has been discussed.
- Show enthusiasm for plans that have been made.
- Give the employee an opportunity to make additional suggestions.
- End on a positive, friendly, harmonious note.

POST-APPRAISAL FOLLOW-UP

_____ As soon as the discussion is over, I will record the plans made, points requiring follow-up and the commitments I made. I will provide a copy for the employee. I will also evaluate
- How I handled the discussion.
- What I did well.
- What I could have done better.
- What I learned about the employee and his/her job.
- What I learned about myself and my job.

PERFORMANCE APPRAISAL CHECKLIST

Place a *circle* around the number indicating the importance of your performance appraisal system in achieving the goals listed below. Then, have your employees do the same and compare their responses with yours.

Scale: 5 — Always   4 — Usually   3 — Occasionally   2 — Seldom   1 — Never

Goals		Yours	Employees'
1. Increase employees' understanding of job role and employer's expectations.	5 4 3 2 1	_____	_____
2. Improve employee morale.	5 4 3 2 1	_____	_____
3. Uphold professional standards.	5 4 3 2 1	_____	_____
4. Increase employees' self-awareness of job performance.	5 4 3 2 1	_____	_____
5. Maintain discipline.	5 4 3 2 1	_____	_____
6. Reward superior performance.	5 4 3 2 1	_____	_____
7. Produce competition among employees.	5 4 3 2 1	_____	_____
8. Reinforce boss-employee relationship.	5 4 3 2 1	_____	_____
9. Improve employee performance skills.	5 4 3 2 1	_____	_____
10. Weed out inferior employees.	5 4 3 2 1	_____	_____
11. Increase employees' self-confidence and self-esteem.	5 4 3 2 1	_____	_____
12. Inform supervisors/upper management of employees' performance.	5 4 3 2 1	_____	_____
13. Basis for awards and/or promotions.	5 4 3 2 1	_____	_____
14. Improve supervisor-employee relationship.	5 4 3 2 1	_____	_____
15. Basis for changing financial compensation.	5 4 3 2 1	_____	_____
Other: _____	5 4 3 2 1	_____	_____

KEY STRATEGY: Both supervisor and employee must complete the checklist.

PERFORMANCE EVALUATION

1. Valid

   • Has a job analysis been conducted recently to determine the duties and responsibilities that must be carried out if the job is to be done successfully?

   • Are performance standards based on the results of the job analysis?

2. Consistent

   • Is the system implemented consistently (does a procedure exist)?

   • Is the same system used for all employees?

   • Do people who do the same work get evaluated against the same standards?

   • Are managers trained to use the system?

3. Useful

   • Is the system perceived to be helpful?

   • Is there support from top management?

   • Is the system easy to administer?

Key Point

The use of any decision-making procedure (i.e., test for selection; applications; resumes; performance appraisal forms for use in promotion, demotion, transfer, discipline, termination and salary actions) that has an adverse impact on any protected group is considered discriminatory, UNLESS that decision-making procedure accurately measures the qualifications required for success in the job.

☐ We're OK   ☐ Review   ☐ Action needed

☐ Person responsible _____

DOCUMENTATION CHECKLIST

Directions: Use this checklist to ensure that you have included all important components of relevant documentation.

Date _____   Employee _____

Actions	Date(s)
☐ 1. Copies of previous performance appraisal	_____
☐ 2. Documented evidence of performance problem	_____
☐ 3. Verbal warning	_____
☐ 4. Written warning	_____
☐ 5. Personal interview(s)	_____
☐ 6. Remedial actions:	
• Type _____	_____
• Attempted _____	_____
• Documented _____	_____
☐ 7. Consequences interview	_____
☐ 8. Check with personnel department	_____
☐ 9. Check with next upper management level	_____
☐ 10. Check with legal department or other legal resource	_____
☐ 11. Termination notification	_____
☐ 12. Termination interview	_____
☐ 13. Explain rights	_____
☐ 14. Exit interview	_____
☐ 15. Debriefing with staff	_____

Contracting with Employee's Action Plan

Employee name _____

_____   _____
               Date   Job title

_____   _____
               Time   Meeting place

Specific problem to be addressed:

Strategy:

Action steps (expectations):

Timetable:

HANDLING PROBLEM EMPLOYEES

Establish Misconduct Policy

Examples:
1. Theft over $10
2. Sexual harassment
3. Major insubordination
4. Obscene/abusive language
5. Asleep on the job
6. Leaving job without permission

1. ORAL NOTICE *Tell 'em...*	2. WRITTEN NOTICE *Tell 'em what you told 'em...*
3. SUSPENSION (Final written notice)	4. TERMINATION

- Discipline is at management's discretion based on employee's position, employment record and mitigating circumstances

- Similar instances of misconduct will be handled on an individual basis

Tips for Discipline

- Fairness
- Open-mindedness
- Timeliness
- Consistency
- Objectivity
- Documentation
- Communication
- Progression

☐ We're OK   ☐ Review   ☐ Action needed

☐ Person responsible _____

How to Get the Employee to Talk

1. Inform the employee, "This position is important to our company, and we feel we must make the best possible decision."

2. Ask the employee, "Does that make sense to you? Do you agree? What do you think we should do?"

3. Continue with the employee, "The more information we have, the better decisions we can make for our company and for you. Do you agree?"

4. Say to the employee, "I feel it is important to talk directly with your peers. Do you have any problems with that?" (Watch closely for the reaction.)

5. Ask the employee, "When I talk with your co-workers, what will they tell me about ... (start with easy questions)?"

6. State as a final comment, "I don't like surprises! Is there anything you would like to explain now before I talk with your former supervisors?"

WRITTEN WARNINGS — A SHORT COURSE

Before documenting unacceptable performance or behavior, be sure you understand the entire situation. Be sure you can answer the following:

WHO?   Who was involved? Who reported the incident? Who witnessed the incident? Who was affected?

WHAT?   What specifically happened? What were the results of the action or inaction?

WHERE? Where did the incident occur?

WHY?   Why did this incident happen — what procedures or rules weren't followed? What is the employee's reason for the incident or behavior?

WHEN?   When did the incident occur? When was it reported? When was the employee given the proper procedures or rules? When was the employee given any other notices of unacceptable performance?

HOW?   How did this incident happen? What did the employee do or fail to do? How did it affect others or the department? How could the incident have been avoided?

There are some simple rules regarding written warnings. After you have investigated the incident or behavior, use the following as a checklist in preparing your document.

- Prepare a neat and readable written warning.

- Address the warning to the employee, date it and sign it.

- Always give the specific details — who, what, where, why, when, how — of the incident or behavior.

- Avoid subjective statements; emphasize association policies and procedures.

- Offer solutions and state objectives.

- Document the consequences of continued unacceptable behavior, e.g., "... failure to ... will result in further disciplinary action up to and including termination."

CONDUCTING A FIRING INTERVIEW

1. Do your homework.

2. If the situation seems to call for it, have a "friendly witness" present during the session.

3. Give clear, specific reasons for the termination. Put these in writing, signed by both parties.

4. Help the employee realize that once the consequences were explained, continuing the unsatisfactory behavior was the employee's matter.

5. Focus the termination on unacceptable behavior, not the person.

6. If it is applicable, advise the employee of the implications of removing files, equipment or other organizational property, as well as revealing trade secrets to competitors.

7. Not all employees will take termination calmly, although the termination should come as no surprise. If the employee becomes upset, these steps will help:
   a. Listen
   b. Share
   c. Continue
   d. Above all, stay in control of your own emotions. There's no need for you to feel threatened by words — you still work there.
   e. If you are physically threatened and there is no one with you, call in someone else immediately.

8. Know company policies.

9. Let employees know where they stand with you. Will you provide references? A final word: Your anxiety about the termination session is both normal and healthy — it is a sign that you are a caring, feeling person, involved with a difficult task.

10. Help employees realize that termination is painful for everyone; you and the organization would like everyone to succeed — and you wish them well.

☐ We're OK   ☐ Review   ☐ Action needed

☐ Person responsible _____

INDEX

Buy two, get one free!

Each of our handbook series (LIFESTYLE, COMMUNICATION, PRODUCTIVITY, and LEADERSHIP) was designed to give you the most comprehensive collection of hands-on desktop references all related to a specific topic. They're a great value at the regular price of $12.95 ($14.95 in Canada); plus, at the unbeatable offer of buy two at the regular price and get one free, you can't find a better value in learning resources. **To order**, see the back of this page for the complete handbook selection.

1. Fill out and send the entire page by mail to:

   In U.S.A.:
   National Press Publications
   6901 West 63rd Street
   P.O. Box 2949
   Shawnee Mission, Kansas 66201-1349

2. Or **FAX 1-913-432-0824**

3. Or call toll-free **1-800-258-7248** (**1-800-685-4142** in Canada)

Fill out completely:

Name _____
Organization _____
Address _____
City _____
State/Province _____ ZIP/Postal Code _____
Telephone ( ) _____

Method of Payment:

❑ Enclosed is my check or money order

❑ Please charge to:

    ❑ MasterCard   ❑ VISA   ❑ American Express

Signature _____ Exp. Date _____
Credit Card Number

_____

To order multiple copies for co-workers and friends: U.S. Can.
    20-50 copies..$8.50 $10.95
    More than 50 copies...............................$7.50 $ 9.95

VIP# 705-008423-094

DESKTOP HANDBOOKS SERIES

	Qty	Item#	Title	U.S.	Can.	Total
LEADERSHIP		410	The Supervisor's Handbook	$12.95	$14.95	
		418	Total Quality Management	$12.95	$14.95	
		421	Change: Coping with Tomorrow Today	$12.95	$14.95	
		423	How to Conduct Win-Win Performance Appraisals	$12.95	$14.95	
		459	Techniques of Successful Delegation	$12.95	$14.95	
		463	Powerful Leadership Skills for Women	$12.95	$14.95	
		494	Team-Building	$12.95	$14.95	
		495	How to Manage Conflict	$12.95	$14.95	
		469	Peak Performance	$12.95	$14.95	
COMMUNICATION		413	Dynamic Communication Skills for Women	$12.95	$14.95	
		414	The Write Stuff: *A Style Manual for Effective Business Writing*	$12.95	$14.95	
		417	Listen Up: *Hear What's Really Being Said*	$12.95	$14.95	
		442	Assertiveness: *Get What You Want Without Being Pushy*	$12.95	$14.95	
		460	Techniques to Improve Your Writing Skills	$12.95	$14.95	
		461	Powerful Presentation Skills	$12.95	$14.95	
		429	Techniques of Effective Telephone Communication	$12.95	$14.95	
		485	Personal Negotiating Skills	$12.95	$14.95	
		488	Customer Service: *The Key to Winning Lifetime Customers*	$12.95	$14.95	
		498	How to Manage Your Boss	$12.95	$14.95	
		426	The Polished Professional — *How to Put Your Best Foot Forward*	$12.95	$14.95	
PRODUCTIVITY		411	Getting Things Done: *An Achiever's Guide to Time Management*	$12.95	$14.95	
		443	A New Attitude	$12.95	$14.95	
		468	Understanding the Bottom Line: *Finance for the Non-Financial Manager*	$12.95	$14.95	
		483	Successful Sales Strategies: *A Woman's Perspective*	$12.95	$14.95	
		489	Doing Business Over the Phone *Telemarketing for the '90s*	$12.95	$14.95	
		496	Motivation & Goal-Setting *The Keys to Achieving Success*	$12.95	$14.95	
LIFESTYLE		415	Balancing Career & Family: *Overcoming the Superwoman Syndrome*	$12.95	$14.95	
		416	Real Men Don't Vacuum	$12.95	$14.95	
		464	Self-Esteem: *The Power to Be Your Best*	$12.95	$14.95	
		484	The Stress Management Handbook	$12.95	$14.95	
		486	Parenting: *Ward & June Don't Live Here Anymore*	$12.95	$14.95	
		487	How to Get the Job You Want	$12.95	$14.95	

SALES TAX		
All purchases subject to state and local sales tax. Questions? Call **1-800-258-7248**	**Subtotal**	
	Sales Tax (Add appropriate state and local tax)	
	Shipping and Handling ($1 one item; 50¢ each additional item	
	Total	

VIP#705-008423-094

THE PAMPERED CHEF®

THE KITCHEN IS THE
HEART
OF THE
H♥ME
COOKBOOK

RECIPES TO MAKE YOUR KITCHEN THE HEART OF THE HOME

Thank you for purchasing this cookbook. Your investment will contribute to a worthy cause in your community.

At The Pampered Chef, we believe mealtime is prime time, and we believe the kitchen is a very special place. It's where families gather for simple, delicious meals. We hope this cookbook brings your family to the heart of your home—your kitchen. We've included some recipes we developed in our own Test Kitchens as well as some we've collected and adapted.

Your kitchen table can be the place where dreams are shared, values are learned, and hospitality is extended. The meal brings you to the table, but the memories will last long after the plates have been cleared.

So when you prepare *Southwestern Chicken with Salsa* as a dinner entrée or make *Banana Cream Brownie Squares* as a dessert to share along with the conversation, savor the spirit of the table as a gathering place and the kitchen as the heart of your home.

Warm regards,

Doris Christopher

Doris Christopher
Founder and President
The Pampered Chef, Ltd.

TABLE OF CONTENTS

Nutritional Guidelines

Nutritional content of these recipes is based on food composition data in The Pampered Chef data base. Variations in ingredients, products, and measurements may result in approximate values. Each analysis is based on ingredients initially listed and does not include optional ingredients, garnishes, fat used to grease pans, or serving suggestions, unless noted. Recipes requiring ground turkey are analyzed based on 95 percent lean ground turkey. Recipes requiring ground beef are based on 90 percent lean ground beef.

APPETIZERS & SNACKS

No matter what you need—a fresh start to a casual meal, a party food, or an afternoon snack—you'll find plenty of tasty options here. Most of these appetite teasers are easy to prepare and some can be made ahead so you'll have more time for conversation with your guests.

Crostini with Sun-Dried Tomatoes

1 (6-ounce) jar oil-pack sun-dried
    tomatoes
1 (16-ounce) baguette, cut into ½-inch
    slices
½ cup chopped fresh parsley
5 ounces Romano cheese, grated
5 ounces Parmesan cheese, grated

Preheat the broiler. Drain the sun-dried tomatoes, reserving the oil. Chop the tomatoes. Brush 1 side of each baguette slice with the reserved oil. Arrange the slices oiled side up in a single layer on an 11x17-inch baking sheet. Broil until light brown. Sprinkle with the sun-dried tomatoes, parsley, Romano cheese and Parmesan cheese. Broil just until the cheese starts to melt. Serve immediately or at room temperature. Yield: 32 servings

Per Serving: Calories 109; Fat 5 g; Sodium 235 mg; Dietary Fiber 1 g

Tortilla Bites

4 (8-inch) fat-free flour tortillas, cut
    into quarters
1 medium onion, grated
1 (16-ounce) can black beans, drained
1 (8-ounce) jar chunky salsa
    Fat-free sour cream (optional)
    Chopped fresh cilantro (optional)

Preheat the oven to 350°F. Spray 16 muffin cups with nonstick cooking spray. Fit 1 tortilla quarter in each muffin cup. Layer the onion, black beans and salsa in the prepared muffin cups. Bake for 8 to 10 minutes or until heated through. Garnish with sour cream and cilantro. Serve immediately. Yield: 16 servings

Per Serving: Calories 56; Fat <1 g; Sodium 242 mg; Dietary Fiber 2 g

APPETIZERS & SNACKS

Cool Salmon Canapés

8 ounces cream cheese, softened
1 (6-ounce) can chunk salmon, drained, flaked
2 tablespoons mayonnaise
1 small carrot, coarsely shredded
1 tablespoon chopped onion
1 tablespoon snipped fresh dill weed, or 1 teaspoon dried dill weed
2 teaspoons lemon juice
1 teaspoon lemon zest
2 medium cucumbers
  Sprigs of fresh dill weed (optional)

Combine the cream cheese, salmon and mayonnaise in a large mixing bowl and mix well. Stir in the carrot, onion, 1 tablespoon dill weed, lemon juice and lemon zest. Spoon the salmon mixture into a pastry bag fitted with a star tip. Score the cucumbers lengthwise with a fork or zester. Cut into ¼-inch slices. Pipe the salmon mixture onto the cucumber slices. Arrange the canapés on a chilled serving platter. Garnish with sprigs of fresh dill weed. Yield: 25 servings (50 canapés)

Per Serving: Calories 54; Fat 4 g; Sodium 67 mg; Dietary Fiber <1 g

The salmon mixture may be piped onto red bell pepper wedges, celery sticks, party bread, miniature bagel halves or assorted party crackers or into cored cherry tomatoes. Substitute fat-free cream cheese and fat-free mayonnaise for a low-fat appetizer if desired.

Seafood Primavera Squares

2 (8-count) cans refrigerated crescent
   rolls
4 ounces cream cheese, softened
1 cup sour cream
½ cup seafood cocktail sauce
1 teaspoon prepared horseradish
1 (6-ounce) can crab meat, drained,
   flaked
1 cup frozen salad shrimp, thawed,
   rinsed
1 cup finely chopped broccoli
3 green onions, thinly sliced
⅓ cup finely chopped red bell pepper
⅓ cup finely chopped green bell pepper
⅓ cup finely chopped yellow bell pepper

Preheat the oven to 350°F. Unroll the roll dough. Pat over the bottom of an 11x17-inch baking sheet with sides, pressing edges and perforations to seal. Bake for 10 to 12 minutes or until light brown. Let stand until cool. Beat the cream cheese, sour cream, cocktail sauce and horseradish in a large mixer bowl at medium speed until creamy, scraping the bowl occasionally. Spread over the baked layer. Layer with the crab meat, shrimp, broccoli, green onions, red pepper, green pepper and yellow pepper. Chill, covered with plastic wrap, until serving time. Cut into 40 squares. Yield: 40 servings

Per Serving: Calories 72; Fat 5 g; Sodium 157mg; Dietary Fiber <1 g

APPETIZERS & SNACKS

Cool California Pizza

1 (8-count) can refrigerated crescent rolls
8 ounces cream cheese, softened
1 garlic clove, pressed
¼ cup freshly grated Parmesan cheese
¼ cup fresh basil leaves, slivered, or 2 teaspoons dried basil, divided
1 (14-ounce) can water-pack artichoke hearts, drained, cut into bite-size pieces
2 medium plum tomatoes, seeded, chopped
½ cup pitted ripe olives, drained, coarsely chopped

Preheat the oven to 350°F. Unroll the roll dough and separate into triangles. Arrange the triangles in a circle with the points toward the center and the wide ends toward the outside on a 14-inch pizza pan. Pat into a 12-inch circle, pressing the seams to seal. Bake for 12 to 15 minutes or until golden brown. Let stand until cool. Combine the cream cheese and garlic in a medium mixing bowl and mix well. Stir in the Parmesan cheese and half the basil. Spread the cream cheese mixture over the baked crust. Sprinkle with the remaining basil, artichokes, tomatoes and ripe olives. Cut into 10 wedges. Yield: 10 servings

Per Serving: Calories 201; Fat 14 g; Sodium 351 mg; Dietary Fiber 3 g

Pizza Breadsticks

1 (11-ounce) package refrigerated
   French bread dough
1 tablespoon olive oil
2 garlic cloves, pressed
½ cup shredded mozzarella cheese
⅓ cup grated Parmesan or Romano
   cheese
1 teaspoon dried oregano
1 (8-ounce) can pizza sauce

Preheat the oven to 375°F. Unroll the bread dough. Pat the dough over the bottom of a 12x15-inch baking sheet with sides. Brush with the olive oil. Spread the garlic evenly over the prepared layer. Sprinkle with the mozzarella cheese, Parmesan cheese and oregano. Bake for 12 to 14 minutes or until golden brown. Pour the pizza sauce into a microwave-safe dish. Microwave on High for 1 to 1½ minutes or until heated through. Cut the baked layer into long strips with a pizza cutter. Serve with the warm pizza sauce.

Yield: 20 servings

Per Serving: Calories 60; Fat 2 g; Sodium 181 mg; Dietary Fiber <1 g

APPETIZERS & SNACKS

Chili Chicken Appetizer Cheesecake

24 ounces cream cheese, softened
1½ teaspoons chili powder
½ to 1 teaspoon hot pepper sauce
3 eggs
1 cup finely chopped cooked chicken
1 (4-ounce) can chopped green chiles, drained
½ cup chunky salsa
½ cup shredded cheddar cheese
3 or 4 green onions, sliced
1 (16-ounce) package tortilla chips

Preheat the oven to 325°F. Combine the cream cheese, chili powder and hot pepper sauce in a large mixer bowl. Beat at high speed until creamy, scraping the bowl occasionally. Add the eggs, beating until blended. Stir in the chicken and chiles. Spoon into a greased 9-inch springform pan. Bake for 40 minutes or until set. Cool in the pan on a wire rack for 15 minutes. Run a sharp knife around the side of the pan; remove the side. Let stand until cool. Chill, covered, for 3 hours or longer. Arrange the cheesecake on a serving platter. Spread the salsa over the top and sprinkle with the cheddar cheese and green onions. Cut into thin wedges. Serve with the tortilla chips. Yield: 16 servings

Per Serving: Calories 341; Fat 25 g; Sodium 466 mg; Dietary Fiber 2 g

Buttery Swiss Cheese Canapés

16 ounces Swiss cheese, shredded
1 cup butter, softened
1/4 cup chopped green onions
2 tablespoons prepared mustard
2 tablespoons poppy seeds
1 (16-ounce) loaf French or Italian bread, cut into 32 slices

Preheat the oven to 350°F. Combine the cheese, butter, green onions, mustard and poppy seeds in a medium mixing bowl and mix well. Spread some of the cheese mixture on each of the bread slices. Arrange the slices in a single layer on an 11x17-inch baking sheet. Bake for 10 minutes or until bubbly. Yield: 32 servings.

Per Serving: Calories 146; Fat 10 g; Sodium 185 mg; Dietary Fiber 1 g

COOK'S TIP — May chill the cheese mixture and serve with assorted party crackers.

Artichoke Frittata

2 (6-ounce) jars marinated artichoke hearts
4 eggs, beaten
1 cup small curd cottage cheese
1 small onion, chopped
1/8 teaspoon dried rosemary
1/8 teaspoon dried thyme
1/8 teaspoon dried basil
1/8 teaspoon dried marjoram

Preheat the oven to 350°F. Drain the artichokes, reserving 2 tablespoons of the marinade. Chop the artichokes. Combine the reserved marinade, artichokes, eggs, cottage cheese, onion, rosemary, thyme, basil and marjoram in a medium mixing bowl and mix well. Spoon into a greased 8x8-inch baking pan. Bake for 30 minutes or until set and light brown. Cut into 1-inch squares. Yield: 16 servings.

Per Serving: Calories 55; Fat 4 g; Sodium 182 mg; Dietary Fiber 1 g

Savory Glazed Meatballs

1½ pounds lean ground beef
1 (8-ounce) can water chestnuts,
     drained, chopped
⅓ cup dry bread crumbs
1 tablespoon beef bouillon granules
2 eggs, lightly beaten
1 (16-ounce) jar peach preserves
1 (12-ounce) bottle chili sauce
1 envelope onion soup mix

Combine the ground beef, water chestnuts, bread crumbs, bouillon granules and eggs in a medium mixing bowl and mix well. Shape into 1¼-inch balls. Brown the meatballs in a 12-inch skillet sprayed with nonstick cooking spray. Remove the meatballs with a slotted spoon to a medium bowl, discarding the pan drippings. Mix the peach preserves, chili sauce and soup mix in the skillet. Cook over low heat for 5 minutes, stirring constantly. Return the meatballs to the skillet and mix gently. Simmer for 10 minutes or until the meatballs are cooked through, stirring occasionally. Spoon into a chafing dish. Serve with wooden picks. Yield: 48 servings

Per Serving: Calories 62; Fat 1 g; Sodium 243 mg; Dietary Fiber <1 g

Fiesta Roll-Ups

1 (15-ounce) can black beans, drained
8 ounces cream cheese, softened
1 cup sour cream
½ teaspoon seasoned salt
½ teaspoon garlic salt
1 cup shredded Monterey Jack cheese
¼ cup finely chopped red onion
¼ cup chopped pimento-stuffed green olives
5 (10-inch) flour tortillas

Combine the black beans, cream cheese, sour cream, seasoned salt and garlic salt in a large mixer bowl. Beat at medium speed until blended, scraping the bowl occasionally. Stir in the Monterey Jack cheese, red onion and green olives. Spread the bean mixture over 1 side of each of the tortillas; roll to enclose the filling. Chill, tightly wrapped in plastic wrap, for 2 hours. Cut into ¾-inch slices just before serving. Yield: 50 servings

Per Serving: Calories 65; Fat 4 g; Sodium 133 mg; Dietary Fiber 1 g

APPETIZERS & SNACKS

Mushroom Puffs

1 (8-count) can refrigerated crescent rolls
3 ounces cream cheese, softened
1 tablespoon milk
½ (4-ounce) can mushroom stems and pieces, drained, chopped
½ teaspoon prepared horseradish
1 egg, beaten
2 tablespoons poppy seeds

Preheat the oven to 400°F. Unroll the roll dough. Separate into 4 rectangles; seal the perforations. Combine the cream cheese and milk in a medium mixer bowl. Beat at high speed until smooth, scraping the bowl occasionally. Stir in the mushrooms and horseradish. Spread the cream cheese mixture evenly over each rectangle. Roll as for a jelly roll to enclose the filling. Cut each roll into 6 equal slices. Dip the slices in the egg. Arrange cut side down on an ungreased 11x17-inch baking sheet. Sprinkle with the poppy seeds. Bake for 10 to 12 minutes or until puffed and golden brown. Yield: 24 servings

Per Serving: Calories 54; Fat 4 g; Sodium 95 mg; Dietary Fiber <1 g

May freeze baked puffs for future use and reheat in a microwave oven for 30 to 45 seconds.

Crunchy Potato Appetizer Balls

2 cups mashed cooked potatoes
2 cups finely chopped cooked ham
1 cup shredded Swiss cheese
½ cup mayonnaise-type salad dressing
2 eggs, beaten
¼ cup finely chopped onion
1 teaspoon prepared mustard
½ teaspoon salt
¼ teaspoon pepper
3½ cups crushed cornflakes

Preheat the oven to 350°F. Combine the potatoes, ham, cheese, salad dressing, eggs, onion, mustard, salt and pepper in a large mixing bowl and mix well. Shape into 1-inch balls. Roll in the cornflakes. Arrange the balls on a greased 11x17-inch baking sheet. Bake for 30 minutes or until brown. Yield: 15 servings

Per Serving: Calories 199; Fat 7 g; Sodium 706 mg; Dietary Fiber <1 g

APPETIZERS & SNACKS

Honey Garlic Chicken Wings

2 pounds chicken wings
⅓ cup honey
2 tablespoons chicken bouillon
2 tablespoons soy sauce
1 tablespoon lemon juice
½ teaspoon garlic powder
¼ teaspoon ground ginger

Preheat the oven to 425°F. Separate the chicken wings at the joints, discarding the tips. Arrange the chicken in a 9x13-inch baking pan sprayed with nonstick cooking spray. Bake for 10 minutes. Combine the honey, bouillon, soy sauce, lemon juice, garlic powder and ginger in a small mixing bowl and mix well. Pour over the chicken, turning to coat. Increase the oven temperature to 475°F. Bake for 25 minutes longer or until the chicken is cooked through. Yield: 12 servings

Per Serving: Calories 115; Fat 6 g; Sodium 252 mg; Dietary Fiber <1 g

Garden Greek Appetizer

8 ounces cream cheese, softened
8 ounces feta cheese, crumbled
¼ cup plain yogurt
1 garlic clove, pressed
¼ teaspoon pepper
2 medium tomatoes, chopped
1 medium seedless cucumber, chopped
3 green onions, finely chopped
3 pitted ripe olives, finely chopped

Combine the cream cheese, feta cheese, yogurt, garlic and pepper in a large mixer bowl. Beat at high speed until smooth. Spread the cream cheese mixture in a round 10-inch dish. Chill, covered, until firm. Top with the tomatoes, cucumber, green onions and ripe olives. Serve with assorted party breads and crackers. Yield: 12 servings

Per Serving: Calories 129; Fat 11 g; Sodium 279 mg; Dietary Fiber 1 g

APPETIZERS & SNACKS

Hummus with Tomato Relish

Hummus
- 2 pita bread rounds, split
- 1 (16-ounce) can chick-peas
- ¼ cup tahini
- 2 tablespoons olive oil
- Juice of 1 lemon
- 1 garlic clove, pressed
- ½ teaspoon salt
- Lettuce leaves (optional)

Tomato Relish
- 1 small onion, chopped
- 1 medium tomato, chopped
- 1 cup chopped fresh parsley

Preheat the oven to 400°F. For the hummus, cut each pita round into 6 wedges. Arrange the wedges in a single layer on an 11x17-inch baking sheet. Bake for 8 to 10 minutes or until light brown and crisp. Remove to a wire rack to cool. Drain the chick-peas, reserving ¼ cup of the liquid. Combine the reserved liquid, chick-peas, tahini, olive oil, lemon juice, garlic and salt in a blender container or food processor. Process until smooth. Spoon onto a platter lined with lettuce. For the relish, combine the onion, tomato and parsley in a small mixing bowl and mix gently. Spoon around the hummus. Serve with the pita wedges. Yield: 6 servings

Per Serving: Calories 261; Fat 12 g; Sodium 537 mg; Dietary Fiber 6 g

Layered Mexican Bean Dip

1 (16-ounce) can refried beans
½ cup taco sauce or salsa
2 avocados, mashed
2 tablespoons lime juice
2 tablespoons vegetable oil
¼ teaspoon garlic powder
1 (4-ounce) can chopped green chiles,
   drained
1 (2-ounce) can sliced pitted ripe olives,
   drained
1½ cups sliced green onions
2 cups sour cream
1½ cups chopped tomatoes
2 cups shredded cheddar cheese

Combine the refried beans and taco sauce in a 2-quart saucepan and mix well. Cook over medium-low heat just until heated through, stirring constantly. Spread in a 2½-quart shallow dish. Mix the avocados, lime juice, oil and garlic powder in a small mixing bowl. Spread over the bean mixture. Layer the chiles, ripe olives, green onions, sour cream, tomatoes and cheese in the order listed over the prepared layers. Chill, covered, until serving time. Serve with corn chips. Yield: 20 servings

Per Serving: Calories 175; Fat 14 g; Sodium 296 mg; Dietary Fiber 3 g

APPETIZERS & SNACKS

Festive Shrimp Appetizer Spread

8 ounces cream cheese, softened
½ cup sour cream
¼ cup mayonnaise
1 teaspoon minced onion
½ teaspoon Worcestershire sauce
2 (4-ounce) cans shrimp, drained
1 cup seafood cocktail sauce
2 cups shredded mozzarella cheese
1 small green bell pepper, chopped
3 green onions, chopped
1 medium tomato, seeded, chopped

Combine the cream cheese, sour cream, mayonnaise, onion and Worcestershire sauce in a medium mixer bowl. Beat at medium speed until creamy, scraping the bowl occasionally. Spread evenly in a 10-inch round shallow dish. Top with the shrimp. Spread with the cocktail sauce. Top with the mozzarella cheese. Sprinkle with the green pepper, green onions and tomato. Chill, covered, for several hours. Serve with assorted party crackers and/or fresh vegetables.

Yield: 32 servings (about 8 cups)

Per Serving: Calories 84; Fat 6 g; Sodium 174 mg; Dietary Fiber <1 g

Cranberry Chutney

½ (16-ounce) package fresh whole
    cranberries
1 cup sugar
½ cup water
½ cup orange juice
½ cup raisins
½ cup chopped walnuts
½ cup chopped celery
½ unpeeled medium apple, chopped
1½ teaspoons orange zest
½ teaspoon ground ginger

Bring the cranberries, sugar and water to a boil in a 3-quart saucepan; reduce heat. Simmer for 15 minutes, stirring occasionally. Remove from heat. Stir in the orange juice, raisins, walnuts, celery, apple, orange zest and ginger. Spoon into a medium serving bowl. Chill, covered, until serving time. Yield: 16 servings

Per Serving: Calories 100; Fat 2 g; Sodium 5 mg; Dietary Fiber 1 g

APPETIZERS & SNACKS

Creamy Caramel Fruit Dip

8   ounces reduced-fat cream cheese,
    softened
¾   cup packed brown sugar
1   cup reduced-fat sour cream
1   cup 2% milk
1   (4-ounce) package vanilla instant
    pudding mix
2   teaspoons vanilla extract
2   teaspoons lemon juice

Combine the cream cheese and brown sugar in a medium mixer bowl. Beat at medium speed until creamy. Add the sour cream, 2% milk, pudding mix, vanilla and lemon juice, beating well after each addition. Chill, covered, until serving time. Serve with assorted fresh fruit. Yield: 16 servings

Per Serving: Calories 122; Fat 4 g; Sodium 153 mg; Dietary Fiber 0 g

Fiesta Bean Salsa

1 (16-ounce) can red kidney beans,
   drained
1 (16-ounce) can black beans, drained
1 (10-ounce) package frozen whole
   kernel corn, thawed, drained
2 plum tomatoes, chopped
1 (4-ounce) can chopped jalapeños,
   drained
4 teaspoons chili powder
1 tablespoon fresh lime juice
¼ teaspoon salt
1 (16-ounce) package tortilla chips

Combine the kidney beans, black beans, corn, tomatoes, jalapeños, chili powder, lime juice and salt in a large mixing bowl and mix gently. Let stand at room temperature for 1 hour, stirring occasionally. Serve with the tortilla chips.
Yield: 18 servings

Per Serving: Calories 193; Fat 7 g; Sodium 375 mg; Dietary Fiber 6 g

APPETIZERS & SNACKS

Tropical Fruit Salsa

1 (8-ounce) can juice-pack crushed
    pineapple
1 banana, sliced, cut into quarters
½ cup sliced kiwifruit, cut into quarters
¼ cup chopped red or green bell pepper
1 small jalapeño, seeded, chopped
2 green onions, thinly sliced
2 tablespoons snipped fresh cilantro
1 tablespoon fresh lime juice

Combine the undrained pineapple, banana, kiwifruit, red or green pepper, jalapeño, green onions, cilantro and lime juice in a medium mixing bowl and mix gently. Serve with Baked Pita Chips. Yield: 8 servings (2 cups)

Per Serving: Calories 47; Fat <1 g; Sodium 1 mg; Dietary Fiber 1 g

COOK'S TIP Use plastic gloves when working with jalapeños. The juice from the peppers may cause a burning sensation on the skin. May substitute chopped peeled peaches, nectarines or mangoes for the kiwifruit.

Baked Pita Chips

4 pita bread rounds

Preheat the oven to 400°F. Split the bread rounds into halves. Cut each half into 8 wedges. Arrange the wedges in a single layer on an 11x17-inch baking sheet. Bake for 8 to 10 minutes or until light brown and crisp. Yield: 8 servings (64 chips)

Per Serving: Calories 83; Fat <1 g; Sodium 161 mg; Dietary Fiber 1 g

Creamy Red Pepper Dip with Vegetables

1 (7-ounce) jar roasted red bell peppers, drained
1 garlic clove, pressed
1 tablespoon thinly sliced fresh basil
1 cup nonfat sour cream
1 cup nonfat mayonnaise
½ teaspoon Worcestershire sauce
⅛ teaspoon salt
1 large green or red bell pepper, cut into halves
6 ribs celery, cut into 2- to 3-inch pieces
2 carrots, cut into thin slices
2 unpeeled cucumbers, sliced
1½ cups broccoli florets
1½ cups cauliflowerets
2 cups small mushrooms

Pat the red peppers dry and chop. Combine the red peppers, garlic, basil, sour cream, mayonnaise, Worcestershire sauce and salt in a large mixing bowl and mix well. Spoon the dip into the green pepper halves and place on a serving tray. Arrange the assorted vegetables around the dip. Yield: 16 servings

Per Serving: Calories 52; Fat <1 g; Sodium 203 mg; Dietary Fiber 2 g

APPETIZERS & SNACKS

Thai Peanut Dip

1 cup smooth or chunky peanut butter
2 tablespoons soy sauce
2 tablespoons lime juice
2 tablespoons vegetable oil or peanut oil
1½ tablespoons honey
1 teaspoon crushed red pepper flakes, or
   to taste
1 clove garlic, pressed
⅛ teaspoon hot pepper sauce
   Minced fresh cilantro (optional)

Whisk the peanut butter, soy sauce, lime juice and oil in a medium mixing bowl until blended. Add the honey, red pepper flakes, garlic and hot pepper sauce and mix well. Spoon into a small serving bowl. Sprinkle with cilantro. Serve with assorted bite-size fresh vegetables. Yield: 10 servings (1¼ cups)

Per Serving: Calories 189; Fat 16 g; Sodium 384 mg; Dietary Fiber 2 g

Confetti Cheese Ball

8 ounces sharp cheddar cheese, shredded

8 ounces cream cheese, softened

1 (8-ounce) can juice-pack crushed pineapple, drained

1 (4-ounce) jar pimento-stuffed green olives, drained, finely chopped

1 medium green bell pepper, chopped

1 medium onion, finely chopped

¼ to ½ cup saltine cracker crumbs

2 cups chopped pecans, divided

Chopped fresh parsley (optional)

Combine the cheddar cheese, cream cheese, pineapple, green olives, green pepper, onion, cracker crumbs and 1 cup of the pecans in a large mixing bowl and mix well. Chill, covered, for 1 hour. Shape into a ball. Roll in the remaining 1 cup pecans and parsley. Chill, wrapped in plastic wrap, until serving time. Serve with assorted party crackers. Yield: 16 servings

Per Serving: Calories 238; Fat 21 g; Sodium 311 mg; Dietary Fiber 2 g

APPETIZERS & SNACKS

Harvest Popcorn

2 cups canned shoestring potato sticks
1 cup mixed nuts
⅓ cup popcorn, popped
⅓ cup melted butter or margarine
1 teaspoon dill weed
1 teaspoon lemon pepper
1 teaspoon Worcestershire sauce
½ teaspoon garlic powder
½ teaspoon onion powder
¼ teaspoon salt

Preheat the oven to 350°F. Mix the potato sticks, mixed nuts and popped popcorn in a large bowl. Combine the butter, dill weed, lemon pepper, Worcestershire sauce, garlic powder, onion powder and salt in a small bowl and mix well. Pour over the popcorn mixture, tossing to coat. Spread in a 9x13-inch baking pan. Bake for 6 to 8 minutes or until heated through, stirring occasionally. Let stand until cool. Store in an airtight container. Yield: 10 servings (10 cups)

Per Serving: Calories 205; Fat 17 g; Sodium 192 mg; Dietary Fiber 3 g

Rock-Pop Trail Mix

1 (3-ounce) package reduced-fat microwave popcorn
1 cup chopped dried fruit
½ cup raisins
½ cup reduced-fat honey-roasted peanuts
2 tablespoons confectioners' sugar
1 teaspoon ground cinnamon

Microwave the popcorn using package directions. Combine the popped popcorn, dried fruit, raisins and peanuts in a large mixing bowl and mix well. Mix the confectioners' sugar and cinnamon in a small bowl. Sprinkle over the popcorn mixture and stir to coat. Yield: 12 servings (12 cups)

Per Serving: Calories 116; Fat 2 g; Sodium 92 mg; Dietary Fiber 3 g

APPETIZERS & SNACKS

Mexican Munch

1 (4-ounce) can shoestring potato sticks
1 (3-ounce) can French-fried onions
2 cups bite-size corn square cereal
1 cup round toasted oat cereal
1 cup rice noodles
¾ cup Spanish peanuts
⅓ cup slivered almonds
¼ to ⅓ envelope taco seasoning mix
¼ cup melted butter or margarine

Preheat the oven to 250°F. Combine the potato sticks, onion rings, corn cereal, oat cereal, rice noodles, peanuts, almonds and taco seasoning in a large mixing bowl and mix well. Add the butter and toss to coat. Spread in a 9x13-inch baking pan. Bake for 30 minutes, stirring every 10 minutes. Yield: 8 servings (8 cups)

Per Serving: Calories 395; Fat 23 g; Sodium 431 mg; Dietary Fiber 3 g

Sugar Pretzels

¼ cup packed light brown sugar
2 tablespoons butter or margarine
1 tablespoon honey
1 tablespoon corn syrup
⅛ teaspoon baking soda
1 (10-ounce) package miniature bow pretzels

Combine the brown sugar, butter, honey and corn syrup in a microwave-safe bowl and mix well. Microwave on High for 2 minutes, stirring once. Stir in the baking soda. Place the pretzels in a 3-quart microwave-safe bowl. Pour the syrup over the pretzels gradually and stir to coat. Microwave the pretzel mixture on Medium-Low for 3 to 4 minutes, stirring twice. Spread the pretzels in a single layer on waxed paper sprayed lightly with nonstick cooking spray. Let stand until cool. Store in an airtight container. Yield: 10 servings

Per Serving: Calories 161; Fat 3 g; Sodium 126 mg; Dietary Fiber 1 g

Sugared Sour Cream Walnuts

1½ cups sugar
½ cup sour cream
½ teaspoon vanilla extract
16 ounces English walnut halves

Preheat the oven to 150°F. Mix the sugar and sour cream in a 3-quart saucepan. Cook over low heat until the sugar dissolves, stirring frequently. Beat in the vanilla. Add the walnuts, stirring just until coated. Spread the walnuts on an 11x17-inch baking sheet lined with waxed paper. Bake for 2 to 3 hours or until the walnuts are dry and sugary, stirring occasionally to separate the walnuts. Let stand until cool. Store in an airtight container. Yield: 16 servings (4 cups)

Per Serving: Calories 270; Fat 19 g; Sodium 7 mg; Dietary Fiber 1 g

APPETIZERS & SNACKS

Banana Pineapple Smoothies

1 banana, chopped
2 tablespoons frozen pineapple juice
   concentrate
1 teaspoon fresh lemon juice or lime
   juice
1 cup crushed ice

Combine the banana, pineapple juice concentrate and lemon juice in a blender container or food processor. Process until mixed. Add the crushed ice gradually, processing constantly until thickened and smooth. Serve immediately.

Yield: 2 servings

Per Serving: Calories 87; Fat <1 g; Sodium 1 mg; Dietary Fiber 2 g

Breakfast Blizzard

1 (15-ounce) can fruit cocktail
1 cup plain or vanilla yogurt
1 cup orange juice or pineapple juice
1 banana, chopped
6 to 8 ice cubes

Combine the undrained fruit cocktail, yogurt, orange juice, banana and ice cubes in a blender container or food processor. Process until puréed. Serve immediately.

Yield: 4 servings

Per Serving: Calories 170; Fat 2 g; Sodium 36 mg; Dietary Fiber 2 g

Red Velvet Punch

2 quarts cranberry juice
6 (6-ounce) cans pineapple juice
1 (6-ounce) can frozen orange juice
    concentrate, thawed
1 (6-ounce) can frozen lemonade
    concentrate, thawed
1 quart ginger ale

Mix the cranberry juice, pineapple juice, orange juice concentrate and lemonade concentrate in a large container. Chill, covered, for 8 to 10 hours. Pour into a punch bowl. Stir in the ginger ale. Ladle into punch cups.

Yield: 24 servings (4½ quarts)

Per Serving: Calories 110; Fat <1 g; Sodium 5 mg; Dietary Fiber <1 g

APPETIZERS & SNACKS

Hawaiian Lemonade

1 (12-ounce) can unsweetened
   pineapple juice
1 (12-ounce) can apricot nectar
1 (6-ounce) can frozen lemonade
   concentrate, thawed
¾ cup water
2 (7-ounce) bottles ginger ale
   Lemon slices (optional)

Mix the pineapple juice, apricot nectar, lemonade concentrate and water in a large pitcher. Chill, covered, in the refrigerator. Add the ginger ale just before serving. Pour over ice in glasses. Twist a lemon slice over the edge of each glass. Yield: 8 servings (1½ quarts)

Per Serving: Calories 103; Fat <1 g; Sodium 6 mg; Dietary Fiber <1 g

Honey Spiced Tea

1½ cups sugar
1½ cups water
 2 (4-inch) cinnamon sticks
 ½ cup red hot cinnamon candies
 1 (46-ounce) can pineapple juice
 1 (46-ounce) can orange juice
 ½ cup honey
 2 cups strong brewed tea

Combine the sugar, water, cinnamon sticks and cinnamon candies in a 3-quart saucepan and mix well. Simmer over low heat for 30 minutes, stirring occasionally. Stir in the pineapple juice, orange juice and honey. Pour into a large container. Chill for 8 to 10 hours. Discard the cinnamon sticks. Add the tea and mix well. Serve hot or cold. Yield: 20 servings (3¾ quarts)

Per Serving: Calories 173; Fat <1 g; Sodium 4 mg; Dietary Fiber <1 g

Strawberry Blossoms

1 (10-ounce) package frozen
   strawberries in syrup, partially
   thawed
1 (6-ounce) can frozen pink lemonade
   concentrate, thawed
1 pint vanilla ice cream
1 cup milk
4 fresh strawberries (optional)

Combine the undrained strawberries, lemonade concentrate, ice cream and milk in a blender container or food processor. Process until smooth. Pour into glasses. Garnish each serving with a fresh strawberry. Serve immediately. Yield: 4 servings

Per Serving: Calories 315; Fat 9 g; Sodium 87 mg; Dietary Fiber 2 g

APPETIZERS & SNACKS

Coffee Mocha Punch

2 quarts strong hot coffee
½ cup sugar
1 ounce unsweetened chocolate, melted
½ teaspoon vanilla extract
⅛ teaspoon salt
1 quart vanilla ice cream
½ (1-liter) bottle club soda, chilled
2 cups half-and-half
1 cup whipped topping
1 cup chocolate syrup

Combine the coffee, sugar, melted chocolate, vanilla and salt in a large container. Chill, covered, for several hours. Slice the ice cream into cubes. Pour the coffee mixture into a punch bowl. Add the ice cream, club soda and half-and-half and mix gently. Ladle into punch cups. Top each serving with a dollop of the whipped topping. Drizzle the chocolate syrup over the whipped topping.

Yield: 20 servings (1 gallon)

Per Serving: Calories 164; Fat 7 g; Sodium 61 mg; Dietary Fiber 1 g

MAIN DISHES

These specially selected entrées will become the centerpiece for family mealtimes and casual entertaining. You'll get rave reviews from family and friends for serving up great flavor with simple flair.

Asian Beef Noodles

1 pound lean boneless beef top round steak, cut into ¼-inch strips
3 garlic cloves, pressed
2 (½-inch) pieces ginger root, peeled, pressed
2 cups water
2 (3-ounce) packages beef-flavor ramen noodles with seasoning packets, broken
3 cups broccoli florets
2 carrots, sliced
2 green onions with tops, sliced

Heat a 12-inch skillet or wok over medium heat until hot. Spray with nonstick cooking spray. Stir-fry the beef in 2 batches in the hot skillet for 3 to 4 minutes. Remove to a medium bowl. Cover to keep warm. Add the garlic and ginger root to the skillet. Stir-fry for 30 seconds. Add the water. Bring to a boil. Stir in the noodles, contents of the seasoning packets, broccoli and carrots. Bring to a boil; reduce heat. Simmer for 3 minutes or until the noodles are tender and most of the liquid has been absorbed, stirring occasionally. Return the beef to the skillet. Cook just until heated through, stirring frequently. Sprinkle with the green onions. Serve using a slotted spoon. Yield: 6 servings

Per Serving: Calories 269; Fat 8 g; Sodium 664 mg; Dietary Fiber 2 g

MAIN DISHES

Spicy Beef and Asparagus

1 pound beef top round steak, trimmed
1 tablespoon cornstarch
1 tablespoon water
½ teaspoon salt
¼ teaspoon pepper
¼ cup beef broth
1 tablespoon soy sauce
1 tablespoon ketchup
2 tablespoons vegetable oil, divided
1 garlic clove, pressed
12 ounces asparagus, trimmed, cut into 1-inch pieces
1 small red bell pepper, cut into thin strips
1 small onion, cut into small wedges

Freeze the steak until partially firm. Slice the beef against the grain into thin strips. Combine the cornstarch, water, salt and pepper in a large mixing bowl and mix well. Add the beef and toss to coat. Mix the broth, soy sauce and ketchup in a small mixing bowl. Set aside. Heat a wok or 12-inch skillet over high heat until hot. Add 1 tablespoon of the oil. Add the garlic. Stir-fry for 30 seconds. Add half the beef mixture. Stir-fry until the beef is brown, removing the beef to a large bowl with a slotted spoon. Repeat the browning process with the remaining beef. Add the remaining 1 tablespoon oil to the wok. Stir-fry the asparagus in the hot oil for 2 minutes or until tender-crisp. Add the red pepper and onion. Stir-fry for 2 minutes or until the vegetables are tender-crisp. Return the beef to the wok. Stir in the broth mixture. Cook until bubbly, stirring constantly. Cook, covered, for 1 minute longer. Yield: 4 servings

Per Serving: Calories 277; Fat 11 g; Sodium 768 mg; Dietary Fiber 3 g

COOK'S TIP Substitute one 10-ounce package frozen asparagus for the fresh asparagus if desired.

Beef and Spring Vegetables with Pasta

2 pounds beef sirloin, thinly sliced
1 large purple onion, sliced
2 tablespoons vegetable oil or olive oil
8 ounces fresh mushrooms, sliced
2 yellow squash, sliced
2 zucchini, sliced
1 (16-ounce) can chunk-style tomatoes
Salt and pepper to taste
16 ounces angel hair pasta, cooked, drained

Sauté the beef and onion in the oil in a 12-inch skillet until the beef is slightly pink. Add the mushrooms, yellow squash and zucchini. Sauté until the vegetables are tender-crisp. Stir in the undrained tomatoes. Cook just until heated through, stirring frequently. Season with salt and pepper. Spoon over the hot pasta on a large serving platter. Yield: 8 servings

Per Serving: Calories 379; Fat 9 g; Sodium 349 mg; Dietary Fiber 3 g

MAIN DISHES

Red Pepper Beef and Pasta

Roasted Red Pepper Pesto

- ¾ cup drained roasted red peppers
- ¾ cup chopped walnuts
- ⅓ cup lightly packed fresh basil
- 3 tablespoons grated Parmesan cheese
- 4 garlic cloves, peeled
- ½ cup olive oil
  Salt and pepper to taste

Pasta

- 1½ pounds (1-inch-thick) boneless beef top sirloin steak, trimmed
- 10 ounces angel hair pasta or linguini, cooked, drained
- ½ cup chopped drained roasted red peppers
- 1 tablespoon grated Parmesan cheese
  Fresh basil (optional)

For the pesto, combine the red peppers, walnuts, basil, cheese and garlic in a blender container or a food processor fitted with a steel blade. Process until smooth. Add the olive oil gradually, processing constantly until blended. Season with salt and pepper. For the pasta, preheat the grill. Grill the steak over medium-hot coals for 17 to 21 minutes for medium-rare to medium, turning once. Brush each side of the steak with 1 tablespoon of the pesto 5 minutes before the steak is of the desired degree of doneness. Cut the steak diagonally against the grain into thin slices. Combine the pasta with the remaining pesto in a medium mixing bowl and toss to coat. Spoon the pasta onto a serving platter. Arrange the sliced beef around the pasta. Sprinkle the pasta and beef with the red peppers and cheese. Garnish with the basil. Serve immediately. Yield: 4 servings

Per Serving: Calories 878; Fat 53 g; Sodium 670 mg; Dietary Fiber 3 g

To broil, place the steak on a broiler rack in a broiler pan. Broil 3 to 4 inches from the heat source for 16 to 21 minutes, turning once. Brush each side of the steak with 1 tablespoon of the pesto approximately 5 minutes before the steak is of the desired degree of doneness.

Grilled Sirloin and Wild Rice Salad

1 (6-ounce) package long grain and
   wild rice
½ cup fresh lemon juice
⅓ cup olive oil
4 garlic cloves, pressed
   Salt and pepper to taste
1 pound beef top sirloin steak, cut into
   4 equal portions
1 (6-ounce) jar marinated artichoke
   hearts, drained, chopped
8 cups mixed salad greens, torn into
   bite-size pieces

Preheat the grill. Prepare the rice using package directions. Cool to room temperature. Combine the lemon juice, olive oil and garlic in a small mixing bowl and mix well. Season with salt and pepper. Reserve ¼ cup of the olive oil mixture. Sprinkle the steaks with salt and pepper. Grill over medium-hot coals for 10 minutes for medium-rare, turning and basting once with the reserved olive oil mixture. Remove to a platter. Combine the remaining olive oil mixture, rice and artichokes in a large mixing bowl and toss lightly. Arrange the mixed greens on 4 dinner plates. Top the greens with a mound of the rice mixture. Cut the steak into thin strips. Fan the steak strips on top of the rice mixture. Serve immediately. Yield: 4 servings

Per Serving: Calories 617; Fat 33 g; Sodium 1164 mg; Dietary Fiber 4 g

MAIN DISHES

Reuben Loaf

3¼ cups all-purpose flour, divided
1 tablespoon sugar
1 teaspoon salt
1 envelope dry yeast
1 cup (120°F to 130°F) warm water
1 tablespoon butter or margarine, softened
¼ cup Thousand Island salad dressing
4 slices Swiss cheese
1 (6-ounce) package thinly sliced corned beef
1 (8-ounce) can sauerkraut, drained
1 egg white, beaten

Preheat the oven to 400°F. Combine 2¼ cups of the flour, sugar, salt and yeast in a large mixing bowl and mix well. Stir in the warm water, butter and enough of the remaining flour to make a soft dough. Knead the dough on a lightly floured surface for 4 minutes. Roll into a 10x14-inch rectangle. Arrange the rectangle on a lightly greased 11x17-inch baking sheet. Spread with the salad dressing. Layer the cheese, corned beef and sauerkraut over the salad dressing. Fold the sides to the center to enclose the filling and seal the edges. Brush with the egg white. Cut slits in the top. Bake for 25 minutes or until golden brown. Cut into 6 slices.
Yield: 6 servings

Per Serving: Calories 441; Fat 13 g; Sodium 1092 mg; Dietary Fiber 3 g

Broccoli and Beef Calzones

1 pound ground beef
1 (10-ounce) package frozen chopped
    broccoli, thawed, drained
1 cup shredded mozzarella cheese
½ cup chopped onion
½ cup sour cream
¼ teaspoon salt
¼ teaspoon pepper
2 (8-count) cans refrigerated crescent
    rolls, divided
1 egg, beaten

Preheat the oven to 375°F. Brown the ground beef in a 12-inch skillet, stirring until crumbly; drain. Stir in the broccoli, cheese, onion, sour cream, salt and pepper. Simmer for 10 minutes, stirring occasionally. Separate 1 can of the roll dough into 2 long rectangles. Arrange the 2 rectangles on an ungreased 11x17-inch baking sheet, overlapping the long sides ½ inch. Seal the edge and perforations. Press into a 7x13-inch rectangle. Spoon half the ground beef mixture in a 3-inch strip down the center of the rectangle. Fold the sides over to enclose the filling. Seal the edge and ends. Repeat the process with the remaining can of roll dough and remaining ground beef mixture. Brush with the egg. Bake for 18 to 22 minutes or until golden brown. Yield: 8 servings

Per Serving: Calories 378; Fat 22 g; Sodium 612 mg; Dietary Fiber 2 g

MAIN DISHES

Mexican Taco Pie

1 pound ground beef
1 medium onion, chopped
1 envelope taco seasoning mix
½ cup water
3 (10-inch) flour tortillas
1 (16-ounce) can refried beans
1 cup sliced pitted ripe olives, divided
1½ cups shredded cheddar cheese, divided
Salsa (optional)
Sour cream (optional)

Preheat the oven to 350°F. Brown the ground beef with the onion in a 12-inch skillet over medium heat, stirring until the ground beef is crumbly; drain. Stir in the seasoning mix and water. Cook using seasoning mix directions until the liquid is absorbed, stirring frequently. Layer 1 tortilla, refried beans, ½ cup of the ripe olives, 1 tortilla, beef mixture, ½ cup of the cheese and remaining tortilla on a greased 12-inch pizza pan. Bake, covered, for 15 minutes; remove the cover. Sprinkle the remaining 1 cup cheese over the top. Bake for 10 minutes longer or until the cheese melts. Sprinkle with the remaining ½ cup ripe olives. Cut into 6 wedges. Serve with salsa and sour cream. Yield: 6 servings

Per Serving: Calories 461; Fat 21 g; Sodium 1066 mg; Dietary Fiber 7 g

Quick Corn Chowder

½ cup chopped red or green bell pepper
1 small onion, chopped
1 tablespoon butter or margarine
1 garlic clove, pressed
2 (14-ounce) cans chicken broth
1 (15-ounce) can cream-style corn
2 medium potatoes, peeled, cut into
    ½-inch chunks
¼ teaspoon ground pepper
½ cup whipping cream or half-and-half
1 tablespoon chopped fresh parsley

Combine the red pepper, onion, butter and garlic in a 2-quart microwave-safe bowl. Microwave on High for 1½ to 2 minutes or until the vegetables are tender-crisp; stir. Add the broth, corn, potatoes and pepper and mix well. Cover loosely with plastic wrap. Microwave on High for 25 to 30 minutes or until the potatoes are tender, stirring once halfway through the cooking process. Stir in the whipping cream. Microwave on High for 2 to 3 minutes or until heated through. Ladle into soup bowls. Sprinkle with the parsley. Yield: 8 servings (8 cups)

Per Serving: Calories 164; Fat 8 g; Sodium 796 mg; Dietary Fiber 2 g

MAIN DISHES

Chili Chicken Salad

Dijon Dressing
  ¼ cup Dijon mustard
  ¼ cup fresh lemon juice
  2 tablespoons water
  1 tablespoon vegetable oil
  1 cup frozen whole kernel corn, thawed
  ½ cup sliced green onions
Salad
  ½ cup chopped onion
  2 tablespoons chili powder
  2 teaspoons ground cumin
  1 teaspoon water
  ¼ teaspoon pepper
  2 garlic cloves, pressed
  4 (4-ounce) boneless skinless chicken
      breast halves
  6 cups packed sliced romaine

For the dressing, whisk the Dijon mustard, lemon juice, water and oil in a small mixing bowl. Stir in the corn and green onions. For the salad, combine the onion, chili powder, cumin, water, pepper and garlic in a small mixing bowl, mixing until of a pasty consistency. Spread the onion mixture evenly over both sides of the chicken. Arrange in a single layer in a 9x13-inch dish. Chill, covered with plastic wrap, for 20 minutes. Preheat the broiler. Transfer the chicken to a broiler rack sprayed with nonstick cooking spray. Broil for 5 minutes on each side or until cooked through and no longer pink. Divide the romaine evenly among 4 dinner plates. Arrange the chicken over the romaine. Top with the dressing.

Yield: 4 servings

Per Serving: Calories 253; Fat 9 g; Sodium 484 mg; Dietary Fiber 5 g

Favorite Chicken

1 (8-ounce) can whole cranberry sauce
1 (8-ounce) bottle French salad dressing
1 envelope onion soup mix
8 (4-ounce) boneless skinless chicken breast halves
4 cups hot cooked rice

Preheat the oven to 325°F. Combine the cranberry sauce, salad dressing and soup mix in a small mixing bowl and mix well. Spread half the cranberry mixture over the bottom of a 9x13-inch baking dish. Arrange the chicken in a single layer over the prepared layer. Top with the remaining cranberry mixture. Bake for 30 to 45 minutes or until the chicken is cooked through. Serve over the rice.

Yield: 8 servings.

Per Serving: Calories 403; Fat 13 g; Sodium 844 mg; Dietary Fiber 1 g

Grilled Chicken Pesto

6 tomatoes, chopped
2 tablespoons prepared basil pesto
1 tablespoon fresh lemon juice
Salt to taste
3 cups hot cooked angel hair pasta
6 (4-ounce) boneless skinless chicken breast halves, grilled

Sauté the tomatoes in a nonstick 12-inch skillet until soft. Stir in the pesto, lemon juice and salt. Cook just until heated through, stirring constantly. Spoon ½ cup of the pasta on each of 6 dinner plates. Top with the chicken. Drizzle with the tomato pesto sauce. Yield: 6 servings.

Per Serving: Calories 273; Fat 6 g; Sodium 102 mg; Dietary Fiber 3 g

Chicken Diane

4 (4-ounce) boneless skinless chicken
    breast halves
½ teaspoon salt
¼ to ½ teaspoon pepper
2 tablespoons vegetable oil, divided
2 tablespoons butter or margarine,
    divided
3 tablespoons chopped green onions
3 tablespoons chopped fresh parsley
2 teaspoons Dijon mustard
    Juice of ½ lemon
¼ cup chicken broth

Pound the chicken between sheets of waxed paper with a wooden meat mallet until flattened. Sprinkle with the salt and pepper. Heat 1 tablespoon of the oil and 1 tablespoon of the butter in a 12-inch skillet over medium heat until hot. Add the chicken. Cook for 4 minutes per side or until cooked through and no longer pink in the center; do not overcook. Remove the chicken to a medium platter with a slotted spoon, reserving the pan drippings. Cover to keep warm. Add the green onions, parsley, Dijon mustard and lemon juice to the reserved pan drippings and mix well. Sauté for 15 seconds. Stir in the broth. Cook until of a sauce consistency, stirring constantly. Add the remaining 1 tablespoon oil and remaining 1 tablespoon butter. Cook until the butter melts and the sauce is heated through, stirring constantly. Drizzle over the chicken. Yield: 4 servings

Per Serving: Calories 242; Fat 16 g; Sodium 518 mg; Dietary Fiber <1 g

Chicken Parmesan

2 egg whites
1 tablespoon water
1 large garlic clove, pressed
½ cup dry bread crumbs
¼ cup grated Parmesan cheese
1½ teaspoons Italian seasoning
¼ teaspoon salt
4 (4-ounce) boneless skinless chicken breast halves
1 tablespoon olive oil, divided
4 (1-ounce) slices mozzarella cheese
½ cup pizza sauce, heated

Whisk the egg whites and water in a medium mixing bowl until foamy. Stir in the garlic. Mix the bread crumbs, Parmesan cheese, Italian seasoning and salt in a shallow dish. Dip the chicken in the egg white mixture. Coat with the crumb mixture, shaking off the excess. Dip each piece again in the egg white mixture and coat with the crumb mixture. Heat 1½ teaspoons of the olive oil in a 10-inch nonstick skillet over medium-high heat. Add the chicken. Cook for 4 minutes or until golden brown. Add the remaining 1½ teaspoons olive oil to the skillet and turn the chicken. Cook for 4 minutes longer or until the chicken is cooked through and no longer pink in the center. Top each chicken breast with 1 slice of the mozzarella cheese. Reduce the heat to low. Cook, covered, for 2 to 3 minutes or until the cheese melts. Transfer the chicken to a serving platter. Drizzle with the pizza sauce. Yield: 4 servings.

Per Serving: Calories 335; Fat 15 g; Sodium 710 mg; Dietary Fiber 1 g

Grilled Chicken Caesar Pizza

3 (4-ounce) boneless skinless chicken
   breast halves
1 envelope Caesar salad dressing mix
6 tablespoons olive oil, divided
3 tablespoons white wine vinegar
1 (16-ounce) Italian bread shell
1 tablespoon grated Parmesan cheese
8 ounces mozzarella cheese, shredded
3 large leaves romaine, coarsely
   chopped
2 Roma tomatoes, chopped

Place the chicken in a large sealable plastic bag. Reserve 1 tablespoon of the dressing mix. Combine the remaining dressing mix, 5 tablespoons of the olive oil and white wine vinegar in a jar with a tightfitting lid. Cover the jar and shake to mix. Reserve 2 tablespoons of the olive oil mixture. Pour the remaining olive oil mixture over the chicken, tossing to coat. Marinate in the refrigerator for several hours, turning occasionally. Preheat the grill or broiler. Remove the chicken from the bag; discard the marinade. Grill over hot coals or broil for 4 to 5 minutes per side or until cooked through and no longer pink in the center. Cut the chicken into thin slices. Preheat the oven to 425°F. Brush the bread shell with the remaining 1 tablespoon olive oil. Mix the reserved 1 tablespoon dressing mix and Parmesan cheese in a small mixing bowl. Sprinkle over the top. Place the bread shell on a round pizza pan. Bake for 5 minutes or until crisp. Arrange the chicken on the baked bread shell. Sprinkle with the mozzarella cheese. Bake for 4 to 5 minutes or until the cheese melts. Toss the romaine and tomatoes in a medium mixing bowl. Drizzle with the reserved olive oil mixture, stirring until coated. Cut the pizza into 6 wedges. Top each wedge with some of lettuce mixture. Yield: 6 servings

Per Serving: Calories 524; Fat 26 g; Sodium 1032 mg; Dietary Fiber 2 g
Nutrition information includes the entire amount of the marinade.

Chicken and Peach Stir-Fry

4 (4-ounce) boneless skinless chicken
   breast halves
8 ounces fresh snow peas, trimmed
1 (16-ounce) can light sliced peaches
1 tablespoon soy sauce
2 teaspoons cornstarch
½ teaspoon ground ginger
1 (8-ounce) can sliced water chestnuts,
   drained
3 cups hot cooked rice

Spray a 12-inch skillet with nonstick cooking spray. Heat the skillet over medium heat until hot. Add the chicken. Cook for 5 minutes per side or until brown and cooked through. Remove to a platter. Cover to keep warm. Add the snow peas to the skillet. Cook for 3 minutes or until tender-crisp, stirring constantly. Remove to a bowl. Cover to keep warm. Drain the peaches, reserving the juice. Combine the reserved juice with enough water to measure 1 cup. Stir in the soy sauce, cornstarch and ginger. Pour into the skillet. Cook until thickened, stirring constantly. Stir in the peaches and water chestnuts. Cook just until heated through and of a sauce consistency, stirring constantly. Cut the chicken diagonally into ¼-inch slices. Spoon the rice onto a serving platter. Top with the snow peas and chicken. Drizzle with the peach sauce. Yield: 4 servings

Per Serving: Calories 395; Fat 3 g; Sodium 399 mg; Dietary Fiber 6 g

Southwestern Chicken with Salsa

Salsa

  4 medium tomatoes, peeled, seeded, chopped
½ cup snipped fresh cilantro
  2 tablespoons chopped green onions
  1 teaspoon white vinegar
  1 teaspoon fresh lemon juice
¼ teaspoon salt
    Ground pepper to taste

Chicken

¼ cup fresh lemon juice
  2 tablespoons olive oil
  1 tablespoon chopped green onions
  1 teaspoon dried basil
⅛ teaspoon ground pepper
  1 garlic clove, pressed
  4 (4-ounce) boneless skinless chicken breast halves

For the salsa, combine the tomatoes, cilantro, green onions, white vinegar, lemon juice, salt and pepper in a medium mixing bowl and mix gently. For the chicken, combine the lemon juice, olive oil, green onions, basil, pepper and garlic in a large mixing bowl and mix well. Add the chicken and stir to coat. Marinate, covered, in the refrigerator for 20 minutes. Preheat the grill. Drain the chicken, discarding the marinade. Grill over medium-hot coals for 12 to 15 minutes or until the chicken is cooked through and no longer pink in the center, turning once. Serve with the salsa. Yield: 4 servings

Per Serving: Calories 218; Fat 10 g; Sodium 214 mg; Dietary Fiber 2 g
Nutrition information includes the entire amount of the marinade.

Grilled Turkey Breast Steaks

¼ cup soy sauce
¼ cup vegetable oil
¼ cup chicken stock
2 tablespoons fresh lemon juice
2 tablespoons dried minced onion
¼ teaspoon dry mustard
Pepper to taste
Garlic salt to taste
4 (4-ounce) turkey breast steaks,
   ¾ to 1 inch thick

Combine the soy sauce, oil, stock, lemon juice, onion, dry mustard, pepper and garlic salt in a 9x13-inch dish and mix well. Add the turkey, turning to coat. Marinate, covered, in the refrigerator for 5 hours or longer, turning occasionally. Preheat the grill. Drain the turkey and discard the marinade. Grill the steaks over medium-hot coals for 6 to 8 minutes per side or until no longer pink in the center.
Yield: 4 servings

Per Serving: Calories 297; Fat 20 g; Sodium 1410 mg; Dietary Fiber <1 g
Nutrition information includes the entire amount of the marinade.

Turkey Loaf with Garlic Mashed Potatoes

Turkey Loaf

    1 pound lean ground turkey
    ½ cup quick or old-fashioned oats
    ⅓ cup chili sauce or ketchup
    ⅓ cup finely chopped onion
    1 egg, lightly beaten
    1 garlic clove, pressed
    1 teaspoon dried oregano
    ½ teaspoon salt
    ⅛ teaspoon ground pepper

Garlic Mashed Potatoes

    1½ pounds unpeeled potatoes, cut into
        1-inch pieces
    5 garlic cloves, peeled
    ⅓ cup fat-free sour cream
    2 tablespoons skim milk
    2 tablespoons snipped fresh parsley
    ½ teaspoon salt
    ⅛ teaspoon ground pepper

Preheat the oven to 350°F. For the loaf, combine the ground turkey, oats, chili sauce, onion, egg, garlic, oregano, salt and pepper in a large mixing bowl and mix well. Shape into a loaf in a 5x9-inch loaf pan. Bake for 40 minutes. For the potatoes, combine the potatoes and garlic with enough water to cover in a 2-quart saucepan and cover. Bring to a boil; reduce heat. Cook for 8 to 10 minutes or until the potatoes are tender; drain. Remove the garlic, mince and reserve. Mash the potatoes in a large mixing bowl. Stir in the garlic. Add the sour cream, skim milk, parsley, salt and pepper and mix well. Spread the potato mixture over the baked loaf. Bake for 15 to 20 minutes longer or until light brown.

Yield: 6 servings

Per Serving: Calories 264; Fat 5 g; Sodium 673 mg; Dietary Fiber 3 g

COOK'S TIP Prepare the turkey loaf using the directions provided but press into a 9-inch glass pie plate. Bake for 25 minutes. Spread with the potato mixture. Bake for 10 to 15 minutes longer or until light brown.

Pineapple Scallop Kabobs

½ cup pineapple juice
2 tablespoons soy sauce
1 tablespoon lemon juice
White pepper to taste
10 ounces fresh scallops
2 canned pineapple rings
1 cup (1-inch squares) red and green
  bell pepper
8 cherry tomatoes
1 cup cooked white rice

Combine the pineapple juice, soy sauce, lemon juice and white pepper in a large mixing bowl and mix well. Add the scallops and pineapple rings and toss to coat. Marinate, covered, in the refrigerator for 1 hour, stirring occasionally. Preheat the broiler. Remove the scallops and pineapple rings from the marinade; discard the marinade. Cut each pineapple ring into quarters. Thread the scallops, red and green pepper squares, pineapple quarters and cherry tomatoes alternately on 2 skewers. Arrange the skewers on a broiler rack in a broiler pan. Broil for 8 minutes or until the scallops are opaque, turning once or twice. Serve over rice.

Yield: 2 servings

Per Serving: Calories 298; Fat 3 g; Sodium 1616 mg; Dietary Fiber 3 g

Nutrition information includes the entire amount of the marinade.

Italian Basil Shrimp

½ cup olive oil
1½ tablespoons butter or margarine
5 garlic cloves, pressed
1 onion, chopped
½ cup chopped fresh parsley
½ cup chopped green onions
8 ounces mushrooms, cut into halves
1 tablespoon dried basil
¼ teaspoon dried thyme
¼ teaspoon dried oregano
1½ pounds shrimp, peeled, deveined
2 cups whipping cream
9 ounces angel hair pasta, cooked, drained

Heat the olive oil, butter and garlic in a 12-inch skillet over medium heat until the butter melts. Add the onion. Cook until the onion is tender, stirring constantly. Stir in the parsley, green onions, mushrooms, basil, thyme and oregano. Cook for 2 to 3 minutes or until the green onions and mushrooms are tender-crisp, stirring constantly. Stir in the shrimp. Cook until the shrimp turn pink, stirring frequently. Remove the shrimp to a heated platter with a slotted spoon. Cover to keep warm. Add the whipping cream to the skillet and mix well. Cook until thickened, stirring constantly. Return the shrimp to the skillet and mix well. Remove from heat. Let stand for 5 minutes. Spoon the shrimp mixture over the hot pasta on a medium serving platter. Yield: 4 servings

Per Serving: Calories 1017; Fat 78 g; Sodium 545 mg; Dietary Fiber 3 g

Seafood-Stuffed Green Peppers

6	medium green bell peppers
1	teaspoon salt, divided
8	ounces shrimp, steamed, peeled
8	ounces crab meat, flaked
1	cup cooked rice
2	tablespoons chopped pimento
1/2	cup finely chopped celery
1/2	cup finely chopped onion
3/4	cup mayonnaise
1	teaspoon seafood seasoning blend
	Pepper to taste
1/2	cup dry bread crumbs
2	tablespoons butter or margarine

Preheat the oven to 350°F. Cut the tops from the green peppers and discard. Remove the seeds and membranes. Combine the green peppers and 1/2 teaspoon of the salt with enough water to cover in a 4-quart saucepan. Bring to a boil. Boil for 5 minutes; drain. Combine the shrimp, crab meat, rice, pimento, celery and onion in a medium mixing bowl and mix well. Stir in a mixture of the mayonnaise, seafood seasoning blend, remaining 1/2 teaspoon salt and pepper. Spoon the shrimp mixture into the green peppers. Sprinkle with the bread crumbs; dot with the butter. Arrange the stuffed green peppers in a 1 1/2-quart baking dish. Add enough hot water to the baking dish to measure 1/2 inch. Bake for 30 minutes or until heated through. Yield: 6 servings.

Per Serving: Calories 418; Fat 29 g; Sodium 1157 mg; Dietary Fiber 3 g

Spicy Stir-Fried Shrimp

1   large onion, cut into thin strips
3   garlic cloves, pressed
2   teaspoons minced ginger root
2   teaspoons vegetable oil
1   pound large shrimp, peeled, deveined
4   cups snow peas, trimmed, cut
        diagonally into halves
½   cup chicken broth
¼   cup hoisin sauce
1   tablespoon soy sauce
2   teaspoons rice vinegar
1   teaspoon cornstarch
⅛   teaspoon hot pepper sauce
8   ounces vermicelli, cooked, drained
2   tablespoons chopped unsalted roasted
        peanuts

Stir-fry the onion, garlic and ginger root in the oil in a 12-inch skillet over medium-high heat for 2 minutes. Add the shrimp and snow peas. Stir-fry for 1 minute. Whisk the broth, hoisin sauce, soy sauce, rice vinegar, cornstarch and hot pepper sauce in a small bowl. Add to the shrimp mixture. Stir-fry over high heat for 3 minutes or until the shrimp turn pink and the sauce is thickened. Toss the shrimp mixture with the hot pasta in a large serving bowl. Sprinkle with the peanuts just before serving. Yield: 4 servings

Per Serving: Calories 423; Fat 7 g; Sodium 849 mg; Dietary Fiber 7 g

Fiesta Chili Corn Bread

Corn Bread Crust

1 tablespoon vegetable oil
1 (11-ounce) can Mexican-style corn, drained
2 (9-ounce) packages corn muffin mix
⅔ cup milk
2 eggs, lightly beaten

Filling

1 (15-ounce) can chili without beans
1 cup shredded cheddar cheese
1 cup shredded Monterey Jack cheese
½ cup thinly sliced green onions with tops
½ cup chopped drained pitted ripe olives
Sour cream (optional)

Preheat the oven to 350°F. For the crust, coat two 10-inch round baking pans lightly with the oil. Line the bottoms with cooking parchment. Combine the corn, muffin mix, milk and eggs in a large mixing bowl and mix well. Spoon half the batter into each of the prepared pans. Bake for 20 minutes. Cool in pans on a wire rack for 10 minutes. Invert each crust onto a serving platter. For the filling, heat the chili in a 1½-quart saucepan over medium heat until hot, stirring occasionally. Spread the chili evenly over the prepared crusts. Sprinkle with the cheddar cheese, Monterey Jack cheese, green onions and ripe olives. Garnish with sour cream. Cut each into 8 wedges. Yield: 16 servings

Per Serving: Calories 289; Fat 15 g; Sodium 666 mg; Dietary Fiber 1 g

MAIN DISHES

Vegetarian Chili with Rice

1 (16-ounce) can red kidney beans, drained
1 (16-ounce) can Great Northern beans, drained
1 (15-ounce) can diced tomatoes
1 (8-ounce) can tomato sauce
1 cup water
1 medium green bell pepper, chopped
1 medium onion, chopped
2 garlic cloves, pressed
1 tablespoon chili powder
1 teaspoon sugar
½ teaspoon dried basil
2 cups hot cooked rice

Combine the kidney beans, Great Northern beans, undrained tomatoes, tomato sauce, water, green pepper, onion, garlic, chili powder, sugar and basil in a 4-quart saucepan and mix well. Bring to a boil; reduce the heat. Simmer, covered, for 15 minutes, stirring occasionally. Ladle into 4 chili bowls. Top each serving with ½ cup of the rice. Yield: 4 servings

Per Serving: Calories 435; Fat 2 g; Sodium 550 mg; Dietary Fiber 19 g

Quick Chiles Rellenos Bake

3 (4-ounce) cans mild whole green
   chiles, drained
2 cups shredded Monterey Jack cheese
9 (8- or 9-inch) flour tortillas
2 (10-ounce) cans enchilada sauce
1 cup sour cream
   Minced fresh cilantro (optional)

Preheat the oven to 350°F. Split each chile lengthwise into halves and remove the seeds. Arrange 2 pepper halves and about 3½ tablespoons of the cheese near the outer edge of each tortilla. Roll to enclose the filling. Arrange the rellenos seam side down in a greased 9x13-inch baking pan. Whisk the enchilada sauce and sour cream in a small mixing bowl. Spoon over the rellenos. Bake for 30 minutes or until bubbly and heated through. Garnish with cilantro. Yield: 6 servings

Per Serving: Calories 675; Fat 38 g; Sodium 1478 mg; Dietary Fiber 5 g

MAIN DISHES

Pasta with Picante Black Bean Sauce

1 medium onion, coarsely chopped
1 garlic clove, pressed
1 tablespoon vegetable oil
1 (15-ounce) can black beans, rinsed, drained
1 (16-ounce) can stewed tomatoes
1 (8-ounce) can stewed tomatoes
½ cup picante sauce
1 teaspoon chili powder
1 teaspoon ground cumin
¼ teaspoon dried oregano
4 cups hot cooked pasta
⅓ cup shredded Monterey Jack cheese or cheddar cheese
⅓ cup chopped fresh cilantro

Sauté the onion and garlic in the oil in a 12-inch skillet until the onion is tender. Stir in the black beans, undrained tomatoes, picante sauce, chili powder, cumin and oregano. Bring to a boil; reduce heat. Simmer, covered, for 15 minutes, stirring occasionally; remove cover. Cook over high heat until of the desired consistency, stirring frequently. Spoon over the hot pasta on a serving platter. Sprinkle with the cheese and cilantro. Serve with additional picante sauce if desired. Yield: 4 servings

Per Serving: Calories 419; Fat 9 g; Sodium 923 mg; Dietary Fiber 12 g

Angel Hair Pasta with Cream Sauce

1 (27-ounce) can garlic and herb
   spaghetti sauce
1 cup half-and-half
1 garlic clove, pressed
½ teaspoon salt
¼ teaspoon freshly ground pepper
⅛ teaspoon ground nutmeg
8 ounces angel hair pasta
¼ cup freshly grated Parmesan cheese
2 tablespoons finely chopped fresh basil

Whisk the spaghetti sauce, half-and-half, garlic, salt, pepper and nutmeg in a 3-quart saucepan. Simmer over low heat until heated through, stirring frequently; do not boil. Cook the pasta using package directions; drain. Toss the spaghetti sauce mixture, cheese and basil gently with the pasta in a medium serving bowl. Serve immediately. Yield: 4 servings

Per Serving: Calories 433; Fat 14 g; Sodium 1242 mg; Dietary Fiber 6 g

MAIN DISHES

Pasta Frittata

¾ cup chopped red bell pepper
½ cup chopped onion
2 tablespoons butter or margarine
2 cups cooked macaroni or spaghetti
5 eggs
⅓ cup milk
2 tablespoons grated Parmesan cheese
1 teaspoon dried basil
½ teaspoon salt
¼ teaspoon pepper
  Chopped fresh parsley (optional)
½ cup shredded sharp cheddar cheese

Preheat the oven to 400°F. Sauté the red pepper and onion in the butter in a 10-inch ovenproof skillet for 5 minutes. Stir in the pasta. Cook for 3 minutes, stirring frequently. Remove from heat. Whisk the eggs, milk, Parmesan cheese, basil, salt, pepper and parsley in a medium mixing bowl until mixed. Pour over the pasta mixture. Cook over low heat for 5 minutes or until the eggs are almost set, lifting the edge with a spatula to allow the uncooked portion to run under the cooked portion. Bake for 5 minutes. Sprinkle with the cheddar cheese. Bake for 3 to 5 minutes longer or until the cheese melts and the eggs are set. Let stand for 5 minutes before cutting into wedges. Yield: 4 servings

Per Serving: Calories 341; Fat 19 g; Sodium 586 mg; Dietary Fiber 2 g

Summer Vegetable Lasagna

1 (10-ounce) package frozen chopped
    spinach, thawed, drained
1 cup shredded carrots
1 cup ricotta cheese
½ cup grated Parmesan cheese
1 egg, lightly beaten
3 tablespoons butter or margarine
¼ cup all-purpose flour
2 cups milk
2 tablespoons tomato paste
¼ teaspoon salt
⅛ teaspoon ground white pepper
6 lasagna noodles, cooked, drained
2 cups shredded mozzarella cheese

Squeeze the moisture from the spinach. Combine the spinach, carrots, ricotta cheese, Parmesan cheese and egg in a medium mixing bowl and mix well. Place the butter in a 4-cup microwave-safe bowl. Microwave on High until melted. Stir in the flour until blended. Whisk in the milk gradually. Microwave on High for 5 to 7 minutes or until thickened, stirring twice. Stir in the tomato paste, salt and white pepper. Spread ½ cup of the tomato mixture over the bottom of a 9x9-inch microwave-safe dish. Layer 2 of the noodles that have been cut to fit the dish, ⅓ of the spinach mixture, ⅓ of the remaining tomato mixture and ⅓ of the mozzarella cheese in the prepared dish. Repeat the layers. Top with the remaining noodles, remaining spinach mixture and remaining tomato mixture. Microwave, covered with waxed paper, on High for 10 to 13 minutes or until heated through, rotating the dish halfway through the cooking process. Sprinkle with the remaining mozzarella cheese. Let stand, covered loosely with foil, for 10 minutes before serving. Yield: 6 servings

Per Serving: Calories 449; Fat 26 g; Sodium 621 mg; Dietary Fiber 3 g

MAIN DISHES

Stuffed Mushroom Spinach Pizza

1 (10-ounce) package frozen chopped
  spinach, thawed, drained
4 ounces fresh whole mushrooms,
  coarsely chopped
½ cup pizza sauce
¼ cup plus 2 tablespoons freshly grated
  Parmesan cheese, divided
1 or 2 garlic cloves, pressed
  Salt and ground pepper to taste
1 (10-ounce) package refrigerated pizza
  dough
2 cups shredded mozzarella cheese,
  divided
2 plum tomatoes, thinly sliced

Preheat the oven to 425°F. Squeeze the moisture from the spinach. Combine the spinach, mushrooms, pizza sauce, ¼ cup of the Parmesan cheese and garlic in a medium mixing bowl and mix well. Season with salt and pepper. Unroll the pizza dough. Roll into a 10x14-inch rectangle on a lightly floured surface. Fit into an 8x12-inch baking dish with sides of the dough extending evenly over the sides of the dish and press lightly. Sprinkle with 1 cup of the mozzarella cheese. Layer with the spinach mixture, remaining 1 cup mozzarella cheese and tomatoes. Make a diagonal slit in the dough at each corner. Bring the sides of the dough together at the center and twist to seal. Sprinkle with the remaining 2 tablespoons Parmesan cheese. Bake for 15 to 20 minutes or until golden brown. Yield: 4 servings

Per Serving: Calories 407; Fat 18 g; Sodium 943 mg; Dietary Fiber 4 g

BREAKFAST & BRUNCH

A special breakfast or a leisurely brunch has become a favorite way to start the weekend. Whether you're scrambling fresh eggs, flipping hot pancakes, or baking a luscious coffee cake, these delightful recipes are sure to please everyone.

Breakfast Pie

1 (8-count) can refrigerated crescent
    rolls
8 ounces chopped cooked ham or
    sausage
1 cup frozen hash brown potatoes
1 cup shredded sharp cheddar cheese
½ cup chopped onion
¼ cup chopped green bell pepper
1 (4-ounce) can sliced mushrooms,
    drained
5 eggs
¼ cup milk
¼ teaspoon salt
⅛ teaspoon pepper
2 tablespoons grated Parmesan cheese

Preheat the oven to 375°F. Unroll the roll dough. Separate into 8 triangles. Pat the dough over the bottom and up the side of an ungreased 12-inch pizza pan, pressing the edges and perforations to seal. Sprinkle with the ham, hash brown potatoes, cheddar cheese, onion, green pepper and mushrooms. Whisk the eggs, milk, salt and pepper in a small bowl. Pour over the prepared layers. Sprinkle with the Parmesan cheese. Bake for 25 to 30 minutes or until a knife inserted in the center comes out clean. Yield: 8 servings

Per Serving: Calories 292; Fat 16 g; Sodium 891 mg; Dietary Fiber 1 g

BREAKFAST & BRUNCH

Chicken Club Brunch Ring

1 cup mayonnaise

2 tablespoons Dijon mustard

2 tablespoons snipped fresh parsley

1 tablespoon finely chopped onion

1 (10-ounce) can chunk white chicken, drained, flaked

4 slices crisp-fried bacon, chopped

1 cup finely shredded Swiss cheese, divided

2 (8-count) cans refrigerated crescent rolls

1 or 2 large plum tomatoes, thinly sliced, cut into halves

1 medium red bell pepper

2 cups shredded lettuce

Preheat the oven to 375°F. Combine the mayonnaise, Dijon mustard, parsley and onion in a medium mixing bowl and mix well. Reserve ⅓ cup and chill the remaining mayonnaise mixture. Combine the reserved ⅓ cup mayonnaise mixture, chicken, bacon and ¾ cup of the cheese in a large mixing bowl and mix well. Unroll the roll dough. Separate into 16 triangles. Arrange the triangles in a circle with the wide ends of the triangles overlapping in the center and the points facing the outer edge on a 14-inch pizza pan, leaving a 5-inch-diameter opening in the center of the pan. Spoon the chicken mixture onto the widest end of each triangle. Bring the outside points of the triangles up over the filling and tuck under the wide ends of the triangles. (The filling will not be completely covered.) Arrange 1 tomato half in each of the pastry openings. Bake for 20 to 25 minutes or until golden brown. Remove from oven. Sprinkle with the remaining ¼ cup cheese. Place the ring on a serving platter. Cut the top from the red pepper and discard. Remove the membranes and seeds. Cut the edge of the red pepper in a V-shaped pattern with a sharp knife. Spoon the chilled mayonnaise mixture into the red pepper. Place in the center of the ring. Arrange the lettuce around the red pepper. Yield: 8 servings

Per Serving: Calories 547; Fat 42 g; Sodium 945 mg; Dietary Fiber 1 g

Easy Cheesy Oven Omelet

1 cup chopped broccoli florets
½ cup chopped red or green bell pepper
¼ cup chopped onion
1 cup shredded cheddar cheese
6 eggs
1 cup cottage cheese
½ cup milk
¼ cup all-purpose flour
½ teaspoon salt
  Ground pepper to taste

Preheat the oven to 425°F. Sprinkle the broccoli, red pepper and onion over the bottom of a lightly greased 7x11-inch baking dish. Top with the cheddar cheese. Whisk the eggs, cottage cheese and milk in a large mixing bowl. Whisk in the flour, salt and pepper. Pour over the vegetable mixture. Bake for 20 to 25 minutes or until a knife inserted near the center comes out clean. Let stand for 5 minutes before serving. Yield: 8 servings

Per Serving: Calories 171; Fat 10 g; Sodium 397 mg; Dietary Fiber 1 g

 Add 1 cup chopped cooked ham, crumbled sausage, shrimp or imitation crab meat to the vegetable mixture if desired.

Monterey Strata

4 cups cheese-flavor tortilla chips
2 cups shredded Monterey Jack cheese
2½ cups milk
1 (4-ounce) can chopped green chiles, drained
1 cup chopped onion
6 eggs, beaten
3 tablespoons ketchup
½ teaspoon salt
¼ teaspoon hot pepper sauce

Layer the tortillas chips and cheese in a greased 9x13-inch baking dish. Mix the milk, chiles, onion, eggs, ketchup, salt and hot pepper sauce in a medium mixing bowl. Pour over the prepared layers. Chill, covered, for 8 to 10 hours. Preheat the oven to 325°F. Bake for 50 minutes or until a knife inserted into the center comes out clean. Yield: 8 servings

Per Serving: Calories 289; Fat 18 g; Sodium 712 mg; Dietary Fiber 1 g

Shrimp and Swiss Frittata

4 slices bacon
1½ cups sliced mushrooms
3 green onions with tops, chopped
½ cup half-and-half
4 eggs
1 teaspoon seasoned salt
  Pepper to taste
1 cup shredded Swiss cheese
1 (6-ounce) package frozen salad
  shrimp, thawed, drained
1 tablespoon minced fresh parsley

Preheat the oven to 350°F. Fry the bacon in a 10-inch skillet until crisp. Drain, reserving 1 tablespoon of the pan drippings. Crumble the bacon. Sauté the mushrooms and green onions in the reserved pan drippings until tender. Spoon into a greased 9x9-inch baking dish. Beat the half-and-half, eggs, seasoned salt and pepper in a medium bowl until blended. Stir in the bacon. Pour over the mushroom mixture. Sprinkle with the cheese. Bake for 20 minutes or until puffed and set in the center. Top with the shrimp. Bake for 2 minutes longer. Let stand for 5 minutes before serving. Sprinkle with the parsley. Yield: 4 servings

Per Serving: Calories 325; Fat 23 g; Sodium 568 mg; Dietary Fiber 1 g

BREAKFAST & BRUNCH

Swiss Cheese Scramble

2 cups soft bread cubes without crusts
1¾ cups milk
8 eggs, lightly beaten
¾ teaspoon salt
⅛ teaspoon pepper
2 tablespoons butter or margarine
¼ teaspoon seasoned salt
8 ounces Swiss cheese, sliced
½ cup fine dry bread crumbs
2 tablespoons melted butter or
     margarine
8 slices crisp-fried bacon, crumbled

Preheat the oven to 400°F. Mix the soft bread cubes and milk in a bowl. Let stand for 5 minutes. Drain, reserving the milk. Whisk the reserved milk, eggs, salt and pepper in a medium bowl until blended. Scramble the egg mixture in 2 tablespoons butter in a 10-inch skillet until soft set. Add the bread cubes and mix well. Spoon the egg mixture into a 9x9-inch baking dish. Sprinkle with seasoned salt. Arrange the cheese over the top. Combine the dry bread crumbs and 2 tablespoons melted butter in a small bowl and mix well. Sprinkle over the prepared layers. Top with the bacon. Bake for 10 to 15 minutes or until set.
Yield: 8 servings

Per Serving: Calories 348; Fat 24 g; Sodium 665 mg; Dietary Fiber <1 g

Swiss-Style Muesli

4   ounces cream cheese, softened
2   cups plain yogurt
¾   cup quick oats
¾   cup chopped hazelnuts
½   cup sliced strawberries
½   cup grape halves
½   cup shredded coconut (optional)
⅓   cup raisins (optional)
1   banana, sliced
1   unpeeled apple, chopped
2   teaspoons lemon juice
¾   cup whipping cream
     Sugar to taste

Combine the cream cheese and yogurt in a medium mixer bowl. Beat at medium speed until blended, scraping the bowl. Stir in the oats, hazelnuts, strawberries, grapes, coconut, raisins, banana, apple and lemon juice. Combine the whipping cream and sugar in a chilled medium mixer bowl. Beat at medium-high speed until soft peaks form. Fold into the fruit mixture. Yield: 8 servings

Per Serving: Calories 309; Fat 23 g; Sodium 80 mg; Dietary Fiber 3 g

Summer Fruit Soup

3 cantaloupes, coarsely chopped
2 cups strawberry halves
½ cup orange juice
2 cups vanilla yogurt, divided
1 cup fresh raspberries
8 sprigs of fresh mint

Combine the cantaloupes, strawberries and orange juice in a blender container or food processor. Process until puréed. Add 1½ cups of the yogurt. Process until blended. Pour into 8 soup bowls. Top each serving with 1 tablespoon of the remaining ½ cup yogurt, 2 tablespoons raspberries and a sprig of mint.

Yield: 8 servings

Per Serving: Calories 158; Fat 3 g; Sodium 58 mg; Dietary Fiber 4 g

Sunshine Grits

3 cups water
1 teaspoon salt
1 cup quick grits
1 cup orange juice
¼ cup butter or margarine
4 eggs, beaten
1 teaspoon orange zest
2 tablespoons brown sugar

Preheat the oven to 350°F. Bring the water and salt to a boil in a 3-quart saucepan. Stir in the grits. Cook over medium heat for 3 minutes, stirring constantly. Remove from heat. Stir in the orange juice, butter, eggs and orange zest. Spoon into a greased 1½-quart baking dish. Sprinkle with the brown sugar. Bake for 45 minutes or until a knife inserted in the center comes out clean.

Yield: 8 servings

Per Serving: Calories 188; Fat 9 g; Sodium 383 mg; Dietary Fiber <1 g

BREAKFAST & BRUNCH

Sky High Biscuits with Raspberry Butter

Raspberry Butter
  ½ cup butter or margarine, softened
  ¼ cup fresh or thawed frozen raspberries
Biscuits
  2 cups all-purpose flour
  1 cup whole wheat flour
  2 tablespoons sugar
4½ teaspoons baking powder
  ¾ teaspoon cream of tartar
  ½ teaspoon salt
  ¾ cup butter or margarine
  1 cup milk
  1 egg, beaten

For the raspberry butter, combine the butter and raspberries in a blender container or food processor. Process until smooth. Chill, covered, for several hours before serving. Preheat the oven to 450°F. For the biscuits, mix the all-purpose flour, whole wheat flour, sugar, baking powder, cream of tartar and salt in a medium mixing bowl. Cut in the butter until crumbly. Add the milk and egg, stirring just until moistened. Knead the dough lightly on a lightly floured surface. Pat 1 inch thick. Cut with a 2-inch biscuit cutter. Arrange the biscuits in a greased 9x9-inch baking pan. Bake for 12 to 15 minutes or until brown. Serve warm with the butter. Yield: 15 servings

Per Serving: Calories 247; Fat 17 g; Sodium 393 mg; Dietary Fiber 2 g

Bake the biscuits on a greased baking sheet for crusty biscuits.

Magical Biscuits

1¾ cups flour
1¾ teaspoons baking powder
1¾ teaspoons salt
½ pint whipping cream

Preheat the oven to 450°F. Mix the flour, baking powder and salt in a medium mixing bowl. Shake the whipping cream vigorously. Add to the flour mixture, stirring until a soft dough forms. Pat the dough ½ inch thick on a lightly floured surface. Cut with a 2-inch biscuit cutter. Arrange 1 inch apart on a lightly greased 11x17-inch baking sheet. Bake for 10 to 12 minutes or until golden brown. Serve immediately. Yield: 8 biscuits

Per Serving: Calories 203; Fat 11 g; Sodium 627 mg; Dietary Fiber 1 g

Buttermilk Scones

2½ cups all-purpose flour
1½ tablespoons sugar
 1 teaspoon baking powder
¼ teaspoon baking soda
¼ teaspoon salt
 2 tablespoons butter or margarine
¾ cup buttermilk

Preheat the oven to 425°F. Combine the flour, sugar, baking powder, baking soda and salt in a medium mixing bowl and mix well. Cut in the butter until crumbly. Add the buttermilk, stirring until a soft sticky dough forms. Pat the dough with floured hands ½ inch thick on a well floured surface. Cut with a 2-inch cutter. Arrange the scones on a greased 11x17-inch baking sheet. Bake for 15 minutes or until golden brown. Serve with strawberry jam and whipped cream or butter. Yield: 12 scones

Per Serving: Calories 124; Fat 2 g; Sodium 151 mg; Dietary Fiber 1 g

BREAKFAST & BRUNCH

Praline Biscuits

½ cup butter or margarine, cut into
   12 pieces
½ cup packed light brown sugar
36 pecan halves
   Cinnamon to taste
2 cups all-purpose baking mix
⅓ cup applesauce
⅓ cup milk

Preheat the oven to 400°F. Arrange 1 piece of the butter, 2 teaspoons of the brown sugar and 3 of the pecan halves in each of 12 greased muffin cups. Sprinkle with cinnamon. Heat in the oven until the butter and sugar melt. Combine the baking mix, applesauce and milk in a medium mixing bowl and stir 20 strokes. Drop by spoonfuls over the butter mixture in the prepared muffin cups. Bake for 10 minutes or until golden brown. Invert onto a serving platter immediately. Yield: 12 biscuits

Per Serving: Calories 238; Fat 12 g; Sodium 299 mg; Dietary Fiber 2 g

Herbed Popovers

1½ cups 2% milk
1½ cups all-purpose flour
1 tablespoon melted butter or margarine
½ teaspoon salt
3 eggs
1 tablespoon minced fresh chives
1 tablespoon minced fresh parsley
1 tablespoon minced fresh thyme

Preheat the oven to 450°F. Combine the 2% milk, flour, butter and salt in a medium mixer bowl. Beat at medium-high speed until blended. Add the eggs 1 at a time, beating just until smooth after each addition. Stir in the chives, parsley and thyme gently; add more or less according to taste. Fill 12 greased medium muffin cups ¾ full. Bake for 15 minutes. Reduce the oven temperature to 350°F. Bake for 20 minutes longer or until golden brown. Yield: 12 popovers

Per Serving: Calories 100; Fat 3 g; Sodium 138 mg; Dietary Fiber <1 g

Lemon Cheese Coffee Cake

1 (2-layer) package lemon supreme cake
   mix, divided
4 eggs, divided
1 cup plus 1 tablespoon all-purpose
   flour, divided
1 envelope quick-rising yeast
⅔ cup (120°F to 130°F) warm water
16 ounces cream cheese, softened
¼ cup sugar
1 tablespoon milk
6 tablespoons butter or margarine
1 cup confectioners' sugar
1 tablespoon light corn syrup
1 tablespoon water

Preheat the oven to 350°F. Combine 1½ cups of the cake mix, 2 of the eggs, 1 cup of the flour, yeast and warm water in a large mixer bowl. Beat at medium speed for 2 minutes, scraping the bowl occasionally. Spread in a greased 9x13-inch baking pan. Combine the cream cheese, remaining 2 eggs, sugar, milk and remaining 1 tablespoon flour in a medium mixer bowl. Beat at high speed until smooth, scraping the bowl occasionally. Spread evenly over the prepared layer. Cut the butter into the remaining cake mix in a medium bowl until crumbly. Sprinkle over the top. Bake for 40 minutes or until golden brown and the edges pull from the sides of the pan. Cool in the pan on a wire rack. Chill, covered, for 3 hours or longer. Combine the confectioners' sugar, corn syrup and water in a bowl and mix well. Drizzle over the coffee cake just before serving. Store, covered, in the refrigerator. Yield: 16 servings

Per Serving: Calories 362; Fat 18 g; Sodium 351 mg; Dietary Fiber 1 g

BREAKFAST & BRUNCH

Raspberry Cheese Coffee Cake

Crust

2¼ cups all-purpose flour

¾ cup sugar

1¼ cups butter or margarine, chilled

¾ cup sour cream

2 eggs, lightly beaten

1 teaspoon almond extract

½ teaspoon baking powder

½ teaspoon baking soda

¼ teaspoon salt

Raspberry Filling

8 ounces cream cheese, softened

¼ cup sugar

1 egg

½ cup raspberry preserves

½ cup sliced almonds

Preheat the oven to 350°F. For the crust, lightly grease and flour the bottom and side of a springform pan fitted with a flat bottom. Combine the flour and sugar in a large mixing bowl and mix well. Cut in the butter until crumbly. Reserve 1 cup of the crumb mixture. Stir the sour cream, eggs, flavoring, baking powder, baking soda and salt into the remaining crumb mixture and mix well. Spread over the bottom and 1 inch up the side of the prepared pan. For the filling, combine the cream cheese, sugar and egg in a medium mixing bowl and mix until smooth. Spoon into the prepared crust. Spread the preserves evenly over the cream cheese mixture. Mix the reserved crumb mixture and almonds in a small bowl. Sprinkle over the top. Bake for 55 to 65 minutes or until the filling is set and the crust is golden brown. Cool in the pan on a wire rack. Remove the side of the pan. Store, covered, in the refrigerator. Yield: 16 servings

Per Serving: Calories 369; Fat 24 g; Sodium 303 mg; Dietary Fiber 1 g

COOK'S TIP Substitute your favorite flavor fruit preserves for the raspberry preserves if desired.

Pull-Apart Sticky Bun

¼ cup chopped pecans
½ cup sugar
1 teaspoon ground cinnamon
1 (11-ounce) package refrigerated
   breadsticks
2 tablespoons melted butter or
   margarine

Preheat the oven to 350°F. Combine the pecans, sugar and cinnamon in a medium mixing bowl and mix well. Unroll the breadstick dough and separate into 8 strips. Dip each strip in the butter and coat with the pecan mixture. Starting at the center of a round shallow 2-quart baking dish, loosely arrange the strips in a spiral fashion to form a circle. Sprinkle with any remaining pecan mixture. Bake for 20 to 25 minutes or until golden brown. Cool in the dish for 5 minutes. Invert onto a serving platter. Serve warm. Yield: 8 servings

Per Serving: Calories 200; Fat 7 g; Sodium 262 mg; Dietary Fiber <1 g

BREAKFAST & BRUNCH

Berry Banana Bread

3 cups all-purpose flour
1½ teaspoons ground cinnamon
1 teaspoon baking soda
½ teaspoon salt
¼ teaspoon ground nutmeg
2 cups sugar
1½ cups mashed fresh strawberries
1 cup vegetable oil
1 cup mashed banana
4 eggs, lightly beaten
1 tablespoon orange zest
1 cup chopped walnuts

Preheat the oven to 350°F. Mix the flour, cinnamon, baking soda, salt and nutmeg in a medium mixing bowl. Combine the sugar, strawberries, oil, banana, eggs and orange zest in a large mixer bowl. Beat at medium speed for 2 minutes, scraping the bowl occasionally. Add the flour mixture, stirring just until moistened. Fold in the walnuts. Spoon into 2 greased 5x9-inch loaf pans. Bake for 1 hour or until a wooden pick inserted in the center comes out clean. Cool in the pans for 10 minutes. Remove to a wire rack to cool. Yield: 24 servings

Per Serving: Calories 261; Fat 13 g; Sodium 113 mg; Dietary Fiber 1 g

Low-Fat Cinnamon Apple Muffins

1½ cups wheat bran flakes cereal with raisins
1 cup whole wheat flour
1 tablespoon baking powder
1 teaspoon ground cinnamon
⅛ teaspoon salt
⅓ cup skim milk
3 tablespoons honey
3 tablespoons vegetable oil
1 apple, peeled, grated

Preheat the oven to 400°F. Mix the cereal, whole wheat flour, baking powder, cinnamon and salt in a medium mixing bowl. Whisk the skim milk, honey and oil in a small mixing bowl. Add to the flour mixture, stirring just until moistened. Stir in the apple. Fill 12 paper-lined muffin cups ¾ full. Bake for 25 minutes or until golden brown. Yield: 12 muffins

Per Serving: Calories 114; Fat 4 g; Sodium 199 mg; Dietary Fiber 2 g

BREAKFAST & BRUNCH

German Apple Pancakes

1 cup creamy cottage cheese
6 eggs
½ cup all-purpose flour
¼ cup milk
¼ teaspoon salt
1 cup chopped peeled apple

Combine the cottage cheese, eggs, flour, milk and salt in a blender container or food processor. Process for 1 minute. Stir in the apple. Pour approximately ¼ cup of the batter for each pancake onto a hot lightly greased griddle. Bake until brown on both sides, turning once. Yield: 8 pancakes

Per Serving: Calories 125; Fat 5 g; Sodium 230 mg; Dietary Fiber 1 g

Merry Berry Syrup

1⅔ cups water
⅔ cup sugar
2 tablespoons light corn syrup
2 tablespoons cornstarch
1 (3-ounce) package raspberry gelatin dessert
1 (8-ounce) package frozen raspberries
1 (8-ounce) package frozen blueberries

Combine the water, sugar, corn syrup and cornstarch in a 2-quart saucepan and mix well. Cook over medium heat until thickened, stirring constantly. Remove from heat. Add the gelatin, stirring until dissolved. Fold in the thawed raspberries and thawed blueberries. Serve over pancakes or waffles. Yield: 8 servings

Per Serving: Calories 169; Fat <1 g; Sodium 31 mg; Dietary Fiber 2 g

Whole Grain Pancakes

Whole Grain Mix

- 8 cups whole wheat flour
- 3 cups old-fashioned oats
- 2 cups instant dry milk powder
- 3 tablespoons baking powder
- 1 tablespoon salt
- 2 teaspoons sugar

Pancakes

- 1¼ cups skim milk
- 1 tablespoon honey
- 1 tablespoon vegetable oil
- 1 egg
- 1½ cups Whole Grain Mix

For the grain mix, combine the whole wheat flour, oats, milk powder, baking powder, salt and sugar in a large mixing bowl and mix well. Store in an airtight container. (Makes 13 cups.) For the pancakes, combine the skim milk, honey, oil and egg in a medium mixing bowl and mix well. Add the grain mix, stirring until mixed; the batter will be lumpy. Pour ¼ cup of the batter for each pancake onto a hot lightly greased griddle. Bake until bubbles appear on the surface and the underside is golden brown. Turn the pancakes over. Bake until golden brown. Yield: 10 pancakes

Per Serving: Calories 94; Fat 2 g; Sodium 163 mg; Dietary Fiber 2 g
Nutrition information contains only 1½ cups of the Whole Grain Mix.

BREAKFAST & BRUNCH

Gingerbread Waffles

2 cups flour
1 teaspoon ground ginger
1 teaspoon baking soda
1 teaspoon baking powder
½ teaspoon salt
2 eggs
¼ cup sugar
1 cup buttermilk
½ cup molasses
⅓ cup vegetable oil

Sift the flour, ginger, baking soda, baking powder and salt into a medium mixing bowl and mix well. Beat the eggs in a medium mixer bowl until blended. Add the sugar, beating until creamy. Add the buttermilk, molasses and oil. Beat until blended. Stir in the flour mixture until smooth. Bake in a waffle iron using manufacturer's directions. Serve with butter and syrup or as a dessert with whipped cream. Yield: 8 waffles

Per Serving: Calories 304; Fat 11 g; Sodium 420 mg; Dietary Fiber 1 g

Baked Apple French Toast

1 (16-ounce) loaf French bread
8 eggs
3 cups milk
¾ cup sugar, divided
1 tablespoon vanilla extract
5 Granny Smith apples, peeled, sliced
2 teaspoons ground cinnamon
2 tablespoons butter or margarine

Preheat the oven to 400°F. Cut the bread into 1½-inch slices with a serrated knife. Arrange the slices in a single layer in a lightly greased 9x13-inch baking pan. Whisk the eggs in a large mixing bowl until blended. Whisk in the milk, ¼ cup of the sugar and vanilla. Pour half the egg mixture over the bread. Arrange the apple slices over the bread. Pour the remaining egg mixture over the apples. Mix the remaining ½ cup sugar and cinnamon in a small mixing bowl. Sprinkle over the top. Dot with the butter. Bake for 30 to 35 minutes or until the apples are tender. Let stand for 10 minutes before serving. Serve with maple syrup.

Yield: 12 servings

Per Serving: Calories 290; Fat 9 g; Sodium 322 mg; Dietary Fiber 2 g

COOK'S TIP May be prepared 1 day in advance and stored, covered, in the refrigerator. Bake, uncovered, for 45 to 50 minutes or until the apples are tender. The recipe may be divided into 2 equal portions and each portion baked in a quiche dish or 2-quart baking dish for 20 to 25 minutes.

French Toast with Cranberry Syrup

French Toast

- 1 (16-ounce) loaf French bread, cut into ½-inch slices, divided
- 2 ounces cream cheese, softened
- 2½ cups eggnog
- 8 eggs
- 6 tablespoons melted butter or margarine
- ¼ teaspoon ground nutmeg

Cranberry Syrup

- 1 cup frozen raspberry juice concentrate, thawed
- 1 cup jellied cranberry sauce
- ⅓ cup sugar

For the French toast, arrange half the bread slices in a single layer in a greased 9x13-inch baking dish. Spread with the cream cheese. Top with the remaining bread slices. Whisk the eggnog, eggs and butter in a medium mixing bowl until blended. Pour over the prepared layers and press the bread slices gently. Sprinkle with the nutmeg. Chill, covered, for 8 to 10 hours. Preheat the oven to 325°F. Bake, uncovered, for 30 to 35 minutes or until the center is set and light golden brown. Let stand for 10 minutes before serving. For the syrup, combine the raspberry juice concentrate, cranberry sauce and sugar in a 2½-quart saucepan. Cook over medium-low heat until the sugar dissolves and the syrup is smooth and hot, stirring constantly. Serve with the strata. Yield: 8 servings

Per Serving: Calories 595; Fat 24 g; Sodium 568 mg; Dietary Fiber 2 g

Cheyenne Cheese Bread

6 slices bacon
3¾ cups all-purpose flour
5 teaspoons baking powder
1 teaspoon salt
2 cups shredded Swiss cheese
¼ cup chopped onion
1½ cups milk
2 eggs, lightly beaten

Preheat the oven to 375°F. Fry the bacon in a 10-inch skillet until crisp. Drain, reserving 2 tablespoons of the pan drippings. Crumble the bacon. Combine the flour, baking powder and salt in a medium mixing bowl and mix well. Stir in the bacon, cheese and onion. Whisk the reserved pan drippings, milk and eggs in a medium mixing bowl. Add to the bacon mixture, stirring just until moistened. Spoon into a greased 5x9-inch loaf pan. Bake for 1 hour. Invert onto a wire rack immediately. Yield: 12 servings

Per Serving: Calories 282; Fat 11 g; Sodium 533 mg; Dietary Fiber 1 g

BREAKFAST & BRUNCH

Focaccia

4 to 4¼ cups all-purpose flour, divided
1 envelope quick-rising yeast
1 tablespoon dried basil
1 teaspoon dried thyme
2 garlic cloves, pressed
½ teaspoon salt
1½ cups (120°F to 130°F) warm water
1 teaspoon honey
2 tablespoons olive oil, divided

Combine 2 cups of the flour, yeast, basil, thyme, garlic and salt in a large mixing bowl and mix well. Mix the warm water and honey in a small mixing bowl. Stir into the yeast mixture. Add enough of the remaining flour to make an easily handled dough and mix well. Knead the dough on a lightly floured surface for 8 to 10 minutes or until smooth and elastic, adding any remaining flour to prevent the dough from sticking to the surface. Place in a large greased bowl, turning to coat the surface. Let rise, covered, in a warm place for 20 minutes or until doubled in bulk. Preheat the oven to 375°F. Punch the dough down. Brush an 11x17-inch baking sheet with 1 tablespoon of the olive oil. Pat the dough into a 10x14-inch rectangle on the prepared baking sheet. Brush the surface of the dough with the remaining 1 tablespoon olive oil. Let rise for 5 minutes. Bake for 30 minutes or until golden brown. Yield: 8 servings

Per Serving: Calories 279; Fat 4 g; Sodium 147 mg; Dietary Fiber 2 g

SIDE DISHES

Enjoy the exceptional colors, flavors, and textures within this collection of delicious sides. Choose the freshest fruits and vegetables for a simple salad or a quick stir-fry. Or, combine them with fresh herbs and spices, grains, and cheeses, and watch them take center stage at your dinner table.

Orange Cream Fruit Salad

1 (20-ounce) can pineapple chunks,
    drained
1 (16-ounce) can sliced peaches,
    drained
1 (11-ounce) can mandarin oranges,
    drained
2 apples, peeled, chopped
3 bananas, sliced
1½ cups milk
1 (4-ounce) package vanilla instant
    pudding mix
⅓ cup thawed frozen orange juice
    concentrate
¾ cup sour cream
Lettuce leaves
Mandarin oranges (optional)

Combine the pineapple, peaches, 1 can mandarin oranges, apples and bananas in a large mixing bowl and mix gently. Combine the milk, pudding mix and orange juice concentrate in a large mixer bowl. Beat at high speed for 1 to 2 minutes or until slightly thickened. Add the sour cream. Beat at medium-high speed until blended. Add to the fruit mixture, stirring gently to mix. Chill, covered, until serving time. Spoon the fruit mixture onto lettuce-lined salad plates. Garnish with additional mandarin oranges. Yield: 10 servings

Per Serving: Calories 231; Fat 5 g; Sodium 175 mg; Dietary Fiber 3 g

Autumn Fruit Salad

2 unpeeled medium Granny Smith
   apples, sliced
1 (11-ounce) can mandarin oranges,
   drained
1 cup seedless red grape halves
   Zest of 1 lime
1½ cups miniature marshmallows
1 cup vanilla reduced-fat yogurt
2 tablespoons chopped pecans

Cut the apple slices into sixths. Combine the apples, mandarin oranges, grapes and lime zest in a chilled 3-quart salad bowl and mix well. Add the marshmallows and yogurt and mix gently. Sprinkle with the pecans. Chill, covered, until serving time. Yield: 12 servings

Per Serving: Calories 89; Fat 1 g; Sodium 19 mg; Dietary Fiber 1 g

Winter Fruit Salad with Honey Lime Dressing

Honey Lime Dressing
- ⅓ cup honey
- 3 tablespoons lime juice
- 1½ teaspoons poppy seeds
- ¼ teaspoon lime zest
- ¼ teaspoon salt
- ⅛ teaspoon ground mace or cinnamon
- ¼ cup vegetable oil

Salad
- 1 bunch leaf lettuce, torn into bite-size pieces
- 3 pears, thinly sliced
- 1 tablespoon lemon juice
- 2 cups seedless red grapes
- ½ cup walnut pieces

For the dressing, combine the honey, lime juice, poppy seeds, lime zest, salt and mace in a small mixer bowl. Add the oil gradually, beating constantly at high speed until mixed. Beat until thickened. Store, covered, in the refrigerator. For the salad, line a large serving platter or 8 salad bowls with the lettuce. Toss the pears with the lemon juice in a medium mixing bowl. Arrange the pears, grapes and walnuts over the lettuce. Chill, covered, for up to 1 hour. Drizzle with the dressing just before serving. Yield: 8 servings

Per Serving: Calories 226; Fat 12 g; Sodium 78 mg; Dietary Fiber 3 g

SIDE DISHES

Fresh Mushroom Salad

1½ pounds button mushrooms
½ cup plus 2 tablespoons olive oil
¼ cup lemon juice
6 tablespoons minced green onions
2 tablespoons chopped fresh chives
¼ cup chopped fresh parsley
   Salt and pepper to taste
6 slices crisp-fried bacon, crumbled

Slice the mushrooms, discarding the stems. Combine the mushrooms, olive oil and lemon juice in a medium mixing bowl and mix well. Stir in the green onions, chives, parsley, salt and pepper. Chill, covered, for 1 hour or longer; drain. Add the bacon, tossing to mix. Serve immediately. Yield: 6 servings

Per Serving: Calories 268; Fat 26 g; Sodium 104 mg; Dietary Fiber 2 g

Grecian Garden Toss

Croutons
  ½ (8-ounce) loaf French bread
  ¼ cup Italian salad dressing
Salad
  2 medium cucumbers, thinly sliced
  2 plum tomatoes, chopped
  ½ medium red onion, coarsely chopped
  1 (4-ounce) can pitted ripe olives,
      drained
  ½ cup crumbled feta cheese
  ½ cup Italian salad dressing
    Salt and ground pepper to taste

Preheat the oven to 375°F. For the croutons, cut the bread into 1-inch cubes with a serrated knife. Toss the bread cubes with the salad dressing in a large mixing bowl. Spread in a single layer on an 11x17-inch baking sheet. Bake for 11 to 13 minutes or until golden brown. Cool on the baking sheet for 10 minutes. For the salad, combine the cucumbers, tomatoes, red onion, ripe olives and feta cheese in a chilled 3-quart salad bowl and mix gently. Add the salad dressing, tossing gently to coat. Season with salt and pepper. Serve with the croutons. Yield: 16 servings

Per Serving: Calories 100; Fat 7 g; Sodium 245 mg; Dietary Fiber 1 g

SIDE DISHES

Spinach and Raspberry Salad

Raspberry Dressing
  2 tablespoons raspberry vinegar or red
       wine vinegar
  2 tablespoons raspberry jam
  ⅓ cup vegetable oil
Salad
  8 cups torn fresh spinach
  1 cup fresh raspberries, divided
  ¾ cup chopped pecans, divided
  3 kiwifruit, sliced

For the dressing, whisk the raspberry vinegar and raspberry jam in a medium mixing bowl. Add the oil gradually, whisking constantly until smooth. For the salad, toss the spinach with half the raspberries and half the pecans in a shallow salad bowl. Add the dressing, tossing to coat. Top with the remaining pecans, remaining raspberries and kiwifruit. Yield: 8 servings

Per Serving: Calories 201; Fat 17 g; Sodium 26 mg; Dietary Fiber 4 g

May substitute fresh strawberries, strawberry jam and strawberry vinegar for a flavor change.

Nutty Pineapple Slaw

2½ cups shredded green cabbage
1¼ cups shredded red cabbage
¾   cup chopped red bell pepper
1   (8-ounce) can crushed pineapple,
      drained
1   cup nonfat sour cream
3   tablespoons cider vinegar
2   tablespoons sugar
1   tablespoon dry mustard
⅛   teaspoon salt
2   tablespoons chopped unsalted
      dry-roasted peanuts

Toss the green cabbage, red cabbage and red pepper in a large salad bowl. Combine the pineapple, sour cream, vinegar, sugar, dry mustard and salt in a medium mixing bowl and mix well. Fold into the cabbage mixture. Chill, covered, for 4 hours or longer. Sprinkle with the peanuts just before serving.
Yield: 8 servings

Per Serving: Calories 88; Fat 1 g; Sodium 64 mg; Dietary Fiber 2 g

SIDE DISHES

Roasted Tri-Color Pepper Salad

1 large red bell pepper
1 large green bell pepper
1 large yellow bell pepper
2 tablespoons olive oil
2 tablespoons balsamic vinegar
2 garlic cloves, pressed
½ teaspoon dried basil
¼ teaspoon salt
⅛ teaspoon pepper
⅓ cup thinly sliced red onion

Preheat the broiler. Cut the peppers into halves. Discard the seeds and membranes. Arrange the pepper halves skin side up on a foil-lined broiler rack. Broil 4 to 5 inches from the heat source for 10 to 12 minutes or until the skin is blackened and charred, rotating the peppers as needed. Let stand, wrapped in foil, for 15 minutes to loosen skins. Peel the peppers under cold running water; pat dry. Cut each pepper half lengthwise into quarters. Whisk the olive oil, balsamic vinegar, garlic, basil, salt and pepper in a medium mixing bowl. Add the bell peppers and onion, stirring to coat. Chill, covered, for 1 hour or longer. Yield: 6 servings

Per Serving: Calories 66; Fat 5 g; Sodium 100 mg; Dietary Fiber 1 g

Sweet Potato Salad

1 (8-ounce) can juice-pack pineapple tidbits
1¼ pounds sweet potatoes, peeled, cut into ½-inch cubes
1 (11-ounce) can mandarin oranges, drained
1 apple, chopped
½ cup chopped celery
¼ cup nonfat sour cream
¼ cup reduced-fat mayonnaise
½ teaspoon salt
¼ teaspoon ground ginger
½ cup chopped walnuts

Drain the pineapple, reserving 2 tablespoons of the juice. Steam the sweet potatoes in a steamer over boiling water for 5 to 7 minutes or until tender-crisp; do not overcook. Remove to a colander. Cool under cold running water; drain. Combine the sweet potatoes, pineapple, mandarin oranges, apple and celery in a large salad bowl and mix gently. Mix the sour cream, mayonnaise, reserved pineapple juice, salt and ginger in a small mixing bowl. Fold into the sweet potato mixture until mixed. Chill, covered, for 1 hour or longer. Stir in the walnuts just before serving. Yield: 8 servings

Per Serving: Calories 208; Fat 7 g; Sodium 225 mg; Dietary Fiber 3 g

Quick Caesar Pasta Salad

Dijon Dressing

- ⅓ cup red wine vinegar
- 2 teaspoons Dijon mustard
- 1 garlic clove, pressed
- ⅛ teaspoon sugar
- ⅛ teaspoon coarse salt
- ½ cup olive oil
- Freshly ground pepper to taste

Pasta Salad

- 8 ounces butterfly or bow tie pasta, cooked, drained
- 8 cups torn mixed salad greens
- 2 cups chopped peeled cucumbers
- 1 cup coarsely chopped walnuts
- 2 ounces Parmesan cheese

For the dressing, whisk the wine vinegar, Dijon mustard, garlic, sugar and salt in a medium mixing bowl. Add the olive oil gradually, whisking constantly until slightly thickened. Season with pepper. For the salad, toss the cooked pasta with 3 tablespoons of the dressing in a large salad bowl. Add the salad greens, cucumbers, walnuts and remaining dressing and mix gently. Shave thin slices of the cheese over the salad with a vegetable peeler or grate over the top. Serve immediately. Yield: 8 servings

Per Serving: Calories 372; Fat 26 g; Sodium 219 mg; Dietary Fiber 3 g

<... >

SIDE DISHES

Mediterranean-Style Pasta Salad

Vinaigrette

1/2 cup olive oil

1/4 cup white wine vinegar

1/4 cup chopped green onions

3 garlic cloves, pressed

1 tablespoon dried basil

1 teaspoon dried dill weed

1/2 teaspoon salt

Salad

2 (12-ounce) packages frozen cheese tortellini

1 (8-ounce) can artichoke hearts, drained, cut into quarters

1 large tomato, chopped

1/2 cup crumbled feta cheese

1/2 cup chopped pitted ripe olives

1/2 cup chopped walnuts

For the vinaigrette, whisk the olive oil and wine vinegar in a small bowl. Add the green onions, garlic, basil, dill weed and salt, whisking until mixed. For the salad, cook the pasta using package directions; drain. Combine the pasta, artichokes, tomato, feta cheese, ripe olives and walnuts in a large salad bowl and mix gently. Add the dressing, tossing to coat. Chill, covered, for 8 hours or longer.

Yield: 12 servings

Per Serving: Calories 329; Fat 18 g; Sodium 441 mg; Dietary Fiber 1 g

Company Asparagus and Rice Salad

2 cups water
1 cup long grain white rice
1¼ teaspoons salt, divided
12 ounces fresh asparagus, trimmed, cut
    diagonally into 1-inch pieces
¼ cup olive oil
3 tablespoons lemon juice
1 teaspoon lemon zest
¼ teaspoon pepper
½ cup chopped green onions
¼ cup grated Parmesan cheese
2 hard-cooked eggs, chopped

Mix the water, rice and ¾ teaspoon of the salt in a 3-quart saucepan. Bring to a boil; reduce heat. Cook, covered, for 15 to 20 minutes or just until tender. Remove from heat. Let stand for 5 minutes; fluff with a fork. Cool to room temperature. Steam the asparagus in a steamer for 3 minutes or until tender-crisp. Whisk the olive oil, lemon juice, lemon zest, remaining ½ teaspoon salt and pepper together in a large mixing bowl. Stir in the rice, asparagus and green onions. Spoon into a serving bowl. Sprinkle with the cheese and eggs. Serve warm or at room temperature. Yield: 6 servings

Per Serving: Calories 255; Fat 12 g; Sodium 587 mg; Dietary Fiber 2 g

Wedding Rice Salad

1 cup sliced dried apricots
½ cup currants
¼ cup lemon juice
1 tablespoon pressed garlic
1 tablespoon minced ginger root
1½ teaspoons ground coriander
1½ teaspoons ground cumin
⅓ cup olive oil
4 cups water
2 cups long grain rice
1½ teaspoons salt
1 cup thinly sliced green onions
½ cup slivered almonds, toasted

Combine the apricots and currants in a medium mixing bowl. Add enough hot water to cover. Let stand for 15 minutes to plump; drain. Mix the lemon juice, garlic, ginger root, coriander and cumin in a small mixing bowl. Add the olive oil gradually, whisking constantly until mixed. Combine the water, rice and salt in a 3-quart saucepan. Bring to a boil; reduce heat. Simmer, covered, for 15 minutes or just until tender. Spread the rice in a large shallow serving bowl. Stir in the green onions. Add the dressing gradually, stirring and turning as the dressing is absorbed and the rice cools. Stir in the apricots, currants and almonds. Serve immediately. Yield: 20 servings

Per Serving: Calories 168; Fat 6 g; Sodium 177 mg; Dietary Fiber 2 g

SIDE DISHES

Wild Rice and Cranberry Salad

Cranberry Dressing
- ½ cup white vinegar
- ½ cup cranberry juice
- 2 tablespoons sugar
- 1 tablespoon olive oil
- 1 teaspoon dried basil
- 1 teaspoon salt

Salad
- 1 cup wild rice, cooked, drained, cooled
- ½ cup chopped celery
- ½ cup dried cranberries
- ½ cup chopped green bell pepper
- ¼ cup chopped green onions
- ¼ cup chopped fresh parsley

For the dressing, whisk the white vinegar, cranberry juice, sugar, olive oil, basil and salt in a small mixing bowl. For the salad, combine the wild rice, celery, cranberries, green pepper, green onions and parsley in a medium salad bowl and mix well. Add the dressing, tossing to coat. Chill, covered, for several hours to enhance the flavor. Yield: 6 servings

Per Serving: Calories 257; Fat 3 g; Sodium 418 mg; Dietary Fiber 3 g

Lemon Carrots

4 cups diagonally sliced carrots
1 teaspoon salt
½ cup butter or margarine
½ cup sugar
1 tablespoon lemon juice
2 teaspoons lemon zest

Combine the carrots and salt with enough water to cover in a 2-quart saucepan. Bring to a boil; reduce heat. Cook, covered, until tender, stirring occasionally; drain. Heat the butter in a 10-inch skillet until melted. Stir in the sugar, lemon juice and lemon zest. Add the carrots and mix gently. Cook over low heat until the carrots are glazed, stirring gently and frequently. Yield: 6 servings

Per Serving: Calories 236; Fat 16 g; Sodium 573 mg; Dietary Fiber 3 g

Quick Saucy Peas

1 (16-ounce) package frozen peas
¼ cup water
½ teaspoon dried dill weed
¼ cup reduced-fat sour cream
2 tablespoons creamy French salad
   dressing
1 teaspoon lemon juice

Combine the peas and water in a 2-quart microwave-safe dish. Sprinkle with the dill weed. Microwave, covered, on High for 8 to 10 minutes or until tender; drain. Mix the sour cream, salad dressing and lemon juice in a small mixing bowl. Stir into the peas. Microwave, covered, on Medium-Low until heated through; do not boil. Yield: 4 servings

Per Serving: Calories 138; Fat 5 g; Sodium 202 mg; Dietary Fiber 5 g

SIDE DISHES

Blue Cheese Potatoes

1½ pounds small red potatoes, steamed,
   cut into quarters
2 tablespoons butter or margarine
3 ounces blue cheese, crumbled
⅓ cup whipping cream
1 garlic clove, pressed
   Salt and pepper to taste
¼ cup grated Parmesan cheese

Sauté the potatoes in the butter in a 10-inch skillet over medium-high heat until the potatoes start to brown. Add the blue cheese, whipping cream and garlic and mix gently. Cook over medium-low heat for 5 to 8 minutes or until a thick creamy sauce forms, stirring constantly. Season with salt and pepper. Spoon into an ovenproof serving dish. Sprinkle with the Parmesan cheese. Preheat the broiler. Broil for 2 minutes or until the cheese is brown. Yield: 4 servings

Per Serving: Calories 374; Fat 21 g; Sodium 490 mg; Dietary Fiber 3 g

Cheesy Potatoes

4 medium baking potatoes, peeled,
   thinly sliced
¼ cup butter or margarine
1 garlic clove, pressed
2 green onions with tops, sliced
¼ cup freshly grated Parmesan cheese

Preheat the oven to 400°F. Arrange the potatoes in an 9x13-inch baking dish. Combine the butter and garlic in a small microwave-safe dish. Microwave on High for 30 seconds or until the butter melts; stir. Drizzle the butter mixture over the potatoes. Sprinkle with the green onions and cheese. Bake for 35 to 45 minutes or until the potatoes are tender and light brown. Yield: 4 servings

Per Serving: Calories 230; Fat 14 g; Sodium 242 mg; Dietary Fiber 2 g

Curried Tomatoes

8 ripe medium tomatoes, peeled, cored
1 cup tomato sauce
2 tablespoons currant jelly
2 teaspoons curry powder
3 tablespoons fresh bread crumbs
¼ cup shredded cheddar cheese
8 slices crisp-fried bacon, crumbled

Preheat the oven to 425°F. Arrange the tomatoes cored side up in a 9x13-inch baking dish. Combine the tomato sauce, currant jelly and curry powder in a 1-quart saucepan. Cook over medium heat for 5 minutes, stirring constantly. Spoon over the tomatoes. Sprinkle with the bread crumbs and cheese. Bake for 15 minutes. Sprinkle with the bacon. Serve immediately. Yield: 8 servings

Per Serving: Calories 101; Fat 5 g; Sodium 326 mg; Dietary Fiber 2 g

SIDE DISHES

Garden Stir-Fry Vegetables

2 garlic cloves, pressed
3 tablespoons vegetable oil
2 onions, thinly sliced
Florets of 1 medium bunch broccoli
8 ounces snow peas, trimmed
10 spears fresh asparagus, chopped
4 carrots, sliced
2 yellow squash, sliced
3 ribs celery, chopped
1 red bell pepper, sliced
Chopped fresh herbs to taste (thyme, basil, rosemary, etc.)
½ cup water
1 cup roasted peanuts

Stir-fry the garlic in the oil in a 12-inch skillet. Add the onions. Stir-fry for 1 minute. Add the broccoli, snow peas, asparagus, carrots, squash, celery, red pepper and fresh herbs and mix well. Stir in the water. Simmer, covered, for 3 minutes. Stir in the peanuts. Serve with sweet-and-sour sauce. Yield: 4 servings

Per Serving: Calories 425; Fat 29 g; Sodium 71 mg; Dietary Fiber 12 g

Substitute with fresh vegetables of your choice.

Italian Vegetable Kabobs

1 medium zucchini
1 medium yellow squash
1 small red onion, cut into wedges
1 medium red or green bell pepper, cut
    into 1-inch pieces
4 ounces fresh whole mushrooms
½ cup Italian salad dressing, divided
¼ cup freshly grated Parmesan cheese

Soak 8 wooden skewers in enough water to cover in a large bowl for 30 minutes. Preheat the grill. Slice the zucchini and yellow squash lengthwise into halves. Cut the halves crosswise into ½-inch pieces. Thread the zucchini, yellow squash, red onion, bell pepper and mushrooms alternately on the wooden skewers or metal skewers. Brush the vegetables with half the salad dressing. Grill the kabobs over medium-hot coals for 10 minutes or until the vegetables are tender-crisp, turning occasionally. Remove the kabobs to a serving platter. Brush the vegetables with the remaining salad dressing. Sprinkle with the cheese. Serve immediately. Yield: 8 servings

Per Serving: Calories 101; Fat 8 g; Sodium 176 mg; Dietary Fiber 1 g

 To broil, arrange the kabobs on a broiler rack lightly coated with vegetable oil. Broil 4 to 6 inches from the heat source for 10 minutes or until the vegetables are tender-crisp, turning once.

SIDE DISHES

Couscous Provençal

1½ cups water
1 cup couscous
2 tomatoes, seeded, cut into ½-inch
   pieces
2 medium green onions, minced
¼ cup chopped celery
¼ cup coarsely chopped kalamata olives
   or pitted ripe olives
¼ cup minced fresh mint
5 tablespoons fresh lemon juice
2 tablespoons olive oil
½ teaspoon ground cumin
½ teaspoon salt
¼ teaspoon freshly ground pepper

Bring the water to a boil in a 2-quart saucepan. Stir in the couscous. Remove from heat. Let stand, covered, for 5 minutes. Spoon into a large shallow serving bowl and fluff with a fork to break up any lumps. Cool slightly. Stir in the tomatoes, green onions, celery, olives and mint. Combine the lemon juice, olive oil, cumin, salt and pepper in a jar with a tightfitting lid. Cover the jar and shake to mix. Add to the couscous mixture, tossing to coat. Chill, covered, for 30 minutes or longer before serving. Yield: 12 servings

Per Serving: Calories 85; Fat 3 g; Sodium 134 mg; Dietary Fiber 1 g

Angel Hair Pasta with Vegetables

1 tablespoon olive oil
16 ounces fresh broccoli, cut into
    bite-size pieces
4 ounces fresh mushrooms, sliced
1½ cups chopped canned tomatoes
½ teaspoon dried oregano
½ teaspoon dried basil
¾ cup reduced-fat cottage cheese
¾ cup plain nonfat yogurt
8 ounces angel hair pasta, cooked,
    drained
Pepper to taste
¼ cup freshly grated Parmesan cheese

Heat the olive oil in a 12-inch skillet over medium-high heat until hot. Add the broccoli and mushrooms. Sauté for 5 minutes. Stir in the tomatoes, oregano and basil. Cook, covered, over medium heat until the broccoli is tender-crisp, stirring occasionally. Combine the cottage cheese and yogurt in a blender container or food processor. Process until smooth. Add to the broccoli mixture and mix well. Toss the broccoli mixture with the pasta in a large serving bowl. Season with pepper. Sprinkle with the Parmesan cheese. Yield: 4 servings

Per Serving: Calories 326; Fat 7 g; Sodium 665 mg; Dietary Fiber 6 g

SIDE DISHES

Summer Linguini

4 large tomatoes, chopped
8 ounces Brie cheese, coarsely chopped
1 cup chopped fresh basil
5 garlic cloves, pressed
½ cup olive oil
½ teaspoon salt
½ teaspoon pepper
6 quarts water
1½ pounds linguini
¼ cup freshly grated Parmesan cheese
Freshly ground pepper to taste

Combine the tomatoes, Brie, basil and garlic in a large mixing bowl and mix gently. Whisk the olive oil, salt and ½ teaspoon pepper in a medium mixing bowl. Add to the tomato mixture, tossing gently to coat. Let stand, covered, at room temperature for 1 hour or longer. Bring the water to a boil in a stockpot. Add the pasta. Cook for 8 to 10 minutes or until tender; drain. Toss the hot pasta with the tomato mixture in a large serving bowl. Sprinkle with the Parmesan cheese and pepper to taste. Yield: 8 servings

Per Serving: Calories 585; Fat 24 g; Sodium 393 mg; Dietary Fiber 8 g

Pasta with Pesto

1 pound very ripe tomatoes
1 cup fresh basil, torn
1 small red onion, chopped
3 garlic cloves, pressed
  Salt and pepper to taste
1 cup olive oil
2 cups penne, cooked, drained

Pour boiling water over the tomatoes to cover in a large ovenproof bowl. Let stand for 1 minute; drain. Plunge the tomatoes into cold water in a bowl. Remove the skins and cut into chunks. Combine the basil, onion and garlic in a blender container or food processor. Process until smooth. Add the tomatoes, salt and pepper. Process until of the desired consistency. Stir in the olive oil. Toss with the pasta in a large serving bowl. Yield: 4 servings

Per Serving: Calories 759; Fat 56 g; Sodium 23 mg; Dietary Fiber 13 g

Wild Rice Amandine with Snow Peas

½ cup sliced almonds
¼ cup butter or margarine
8 ounces snow peas, trimmed
6 green onions, cut into diagonal slices
2 cups cooked wild rice
½ cup chicken broth
  Salt and pepper to taste

Sauté the almonds in the butter in a 10-inch skillet over medium-high heat just until the almonds begin to brown. Stir in the snow peas and sliced green onions. Stir-fry for 2 to 3 minutes or until tender-crisp. Add the wild rice and broth and mix well. Stir-fry until the liquid is absorbed. Season with salt and pepper. Yield: 4 servings

Per Serving: Calories 288; Fat 18 g; Sodium 223 mg; Dietary Fiber 5 g

SIDE DISHES

Gingery Rice Pilaf

2 tablespoons butter or margarine
1 tablespoon finely chopped peeled
   ginger root
1 (14-ounce) can chicken broth
1 (4-ounce) can mushroom stems and
   pieces, drained
1 cup long grain white rice
2 green onions with tops, thinly sliced
½ cup frozen green peas

Heat the butter in a 2-quart saucepan over medium heat until melted, stirring constantly. Add the ginger root. Sauté for 1 minute. Stir in the broth, mushrooms, rice and green onions. Bring to a boil; reduce heat. Simmer, covered, for 20 minutes or until the rice is tender. Remove from heat. Stir in the peas. Let stand, covered, for 5 minutes. Fluff with a fork. Yield: 4 servings

Per Serving: Calories 273; Fat 7 g; Sodium 807 mg; Dietary Fiber 2 g

Classic Risotto

4 tablespoons butter or margarine, divided
1 onion, finely chopped
2 cups arborio rice
6 cups canned low-sodium chicken broth, divided
1 cup freshly grated Parmesan cheese, divided
2 tablespoons chopped fresh parsley
Salt and pepper to taste

Heat 2 tablespoons of the butter in a heavy 4-quart saucepan until melted. Stir in the onion. Cook over medium heat for 4 minutes or until tender, stirring frequently. Add the rice and mix well. Cook for 2 minutes, stirring constantly. Heat the broth in a 3-quart saucepan just to the boiling point. Add 1 cup of the broth to the rice mixture. Cook until the liquid is absorbed, stirring constantly. Repeat the process with 3 more cups of the broth. Remove from heat. Let stand, covered, for 20 minutes. Return to heat. Add the remaining 2 cups broth gradually, stirring constantly. Cook over medium heat until the rice is creamy. Stir in ¾ cup of the cheese, the remaining 2 tablespoons butter, parsley, salt and pepper. Spoon into a large serving bowl. Sprinkle with the remaining ¼ cup cheese. Yield: 8 servings

Per Serving: Calories 353; Fat 11 g; Sodium 772 mg; Dietary Fiber 1 g

SIDE DISHES

Savory Brown Rice

1 cup quick brown rice
¾ envelope onion soup mix
2 tablespoons butter or margarine
1 (4-ounce) can sliced mushrooms,
     drained
½ cup coarsely chopped walnuts
2 tablespoons chopped fresh parsley
½ cup shredded sharp cheddar cheese

Cook the brown rice using package directions, adding the soup mix and omitting the salt. Heat the butter in a small saucepan until melted. Add the mushrooms, walnuts and parsley. Sauté until bubbly. Stir the mushroom mixture into the rice. Add the cheese and mix well. Let stand, covered, for 5 minutes before serving.
Yield: 6 servings

Per Serving: Calories 231; Fat 14 g; Sodium 616 mg; Dietary Fiber 2 g

DESSERTS

Everyone has a special fondness for dessert, whether at the end of a meal or in the middle of the day. From comforting cobblers to richly delicious cheesecakes, these irresistible desserts will satisfy every sweet tooth.

Apple and Pineapple Crisp

4 cups sliced peeled apples
1 (8-ounce) can crushed pineapple
1 tablespoon lemon juice
¾ cup packed brown sugar
½ cup old-fashioned oats
1 teaspoon ground cinnamon
1 teaspoon ground nutmeg
½ cup chopped pecans
⅓ cup melted butter or margarine

Preheat the oven to 350°F. Arrange the apples in a 9x9-inch baking dish sprayed with nonstick cooking spray. Mix the undrained pineapple and lemon juice in a bowl. Spread over the apples. Combine the brown sugar, oats, cinnamon, nutmeg and pecans in a bowl and mix well. Stir in the butter. Sprinkle over the prepared layers. Bake, covered with foil, for 30 minutes; remove the foil. Bake for 10 to 12 minutes longer or until crisp. Yield: 8 servings

Per Serving: Calories 273; Fat 13 g; Sodium 87 mg; Dietary Fiber 2 g

DESSERTS

Old-Fashioned Apple Bread Pudding

2 cups chopped peeled apples
3 tablespoons butter or margarine
2 teaspoons ground cinnamon, divided
½ teaspoon ground nutmeg, divided
1 (12-ounce) can evaporated milk
½ cup packed brown sugar
⅓ cup raisins
¼ cup apple juice
3 eggs, lightly beaten
1 teaspoon vanilla extract
4 cups (1-inch) firm-texture bread
　　cubes
½ cup chopped walnuts
2 tablespoons sugar

Preheat the oven to 350°F. Mix the apples, butter, 1 teaspoon of the cinnamon and ¼ teaspoon of the nutmeg in a 3-quart saucepan. Cook over medium heat for 5 minutes, stirring frequently. Add the evaporated milk, brown sugar, raisins, apple juice, eggs and vanilla and mix well. Stir in the bread cubes. Spoon into a greased 8x8-inch baking dish. Mix the remaining 1 teaspoon cinnamon, remaining ¼ teaspoon nutmeg, walnuts and sugar in a small bowl. Sprinkle over the top. Bake for 30 to 35 minutes or until a knife inserted near the center comes out clean. Serve warm with whipped cream. Yield: 6 servings

Per Serving: Calories 420; Fat 19 g; Sodium 257 mg; Dietary Fiber 2 g

Creamy Banana Pudding

¼ cup lemon juice
6 or 7 medium bananas, sliced
3 cups 2% milk
2 (4-ounce) packages vanilla instant pudding mix
1 (14-ounce) can sweetened condensed milk
16 ounces frozen whipped topping, thawed
1 (16-ounce) package vanilla wafers

Drizzle the lemon juice over the bananas in a medium bowl. Whisk the 2% milk and pudding mix in a large mixing bowl for 3 to 4 minutes or until blended and slightly thickened. Add the condensed milk and mix well. Chill for 5 minutes. Fold in the whipped topping. Layer the vanilla wafers, bananas and pudding mixture alternately in a large serving bowl until all of the ingredients are used, ending with the pudding mixture. Store, covered, in the refrigerator until serving time. Yield: 15 servings

Per Serving: Calories 443; Fat 14 g; Sodium 371 mg; Dietary Fiber 2 g

DESSERTS

Banana Cream Brownie Squares

1 (15-ounce) package brownie mix
¾ cup chopped dry-roasted peanuts, divided
3 medium bananas, divided
1 (6-ounce) package vanilla instant pudding mix
1¼ cups cold milk
8 ounces frozen whipped topping, thawed, divided
2 tablespoons grated semisweet chocolate
12 whole strawberries

Preheat the oven to 350°F. Prepare the brownie mix using package directions and adding ½ cup of the peanuts. Spoon into a greased 9x9-inch baking pan. Bake for 25 to 27 minutes or until the edges pull from the sides of the pan. Cool in the pan on a wire rack. Slice 2 of the bananas and arrange in a single layer over the brownie layer. Whisk the pudding mix into the milk in a medium mixing bowl until blended. Whisk just until the mixture begins to thicken. Fold in 2½ cups of the whipped topping. Spread over the bananas. Chill, covered, for 30 minutes. Sprinkle with the remaining ¼ cup peanuts. Cut into 12 squares. Spoon the remaining whipped topping into a pastry bag fitted with a star tip. Pipe some of the whipped topping onto each brownie. Sprinkle with the chocolate. Slice the remaining banana. Top each serving with a strawberry and some of the banana slices. Yield: 12 brownies

Per Serving: Calories 322; Fat 14 g; Sodium 262 mg; Dietary Fiber 2 g

Berries 'n Cream Parfaits

1 envelope whipped topping mix
8 ounces cream cheese, softened
¼ cup plus 3 tablespoons sugar, divided
1 teaspoon vanilla extract
1 (3-ounce) package raspberry gelatin
  dessert
1¼ cups boiling water
2 cups frozen whole raspberries

Prepare the whipped topping using package directions. Combine the cream cheese, ¼ cup of the sugar and vanilla in a medium mixer bowl. Beat at high speed until light and fluffy, scraping the bowl occasionally. Fold in the whipped topping. Dissolve the gelatin in the boiling water in a medium mixing bowl. Add the remaining 3 tablespoons sugar and raspberries, stirring until the mixture begins to thicken. Alternate layers of the gelatin mixture and cream cheese mixture in 6 parfait glasses until all the ingredients are used. Chill for 1 hour before serving. Yield: 6 servings

Per Serving: Calories 378; Fat 16 g; Sodium 172 mg; Dietary Fiber 4 g

DESSERTS

Chocolate Chip Sensation

1 (18-ounce) package refrigerated
   chocolate chip cookie dough
8 ounces cream cheese, softened
⅓ cup sugar
1 (4-ounce) package chocolate instant
   pudding mix
2 cups half-and-half
¼ cup chopped pecans

Preheat the oven to 375°F. Shape the cookie dough into a ball. Place in the center of a 14-inch pizza pan. Pat the dough into a 13-inch circle. Bake for 12 to 15 minutes or until light brown. Cool on the pan for 10 minutes. Remove to a wire rack to cool completely. Combine the cream cheese and sugar in a medium mixing bowl and mix until smooth. Whisk the pudding mix into the half-and-half in a large mixing bowl until blended. Let stand for 5 minutes or until thickened. Arrange the cookie layer on a serving plate. Spread evenly with the cream cheese mixture. Top with the pudding mixture. Sprinkle with the pecans. Chill, covered, until serving time. Cut into wedges. Yield: 20 servings

Per Serving: Calories 224; Fat 13 g; Sodium 168 mg; Dietary Fiber 1 g

Cream Puff-in-a-Pan

1 cup water
½ cup butter or margarine
1 cup all-purpose flour
4 eggs
8 ounces cream cheese, softened
2 (4-ounce) packages vanilla instant
  pudding mix
2 cups milk
12 ounces frozen whipped topping,
   thawed
¼ cup chocolate syrup
  Grated chocolate (optional)

Preheat the oven to 350°F. Bring the water and butter to a boil in a 2-quart saucepan, stirring occasionally. Stir in the flour. Add the eggs 1 at a time, whisking well after each addition. Spread the batter in a greased 10x15-inch baking pan. Bake for 25 minutes. Cool in the pan on a wire rack. Beat the cream cheese in a mixer bowl until smooth, scraping the bowl occasionally. Add the pudding mix and milk. Beat until blended. Spread over the baked layer. Top with the whipped topping. Chill, covered, in the refrigerator. Drizzle with the chocolate syrup. Garnish with grated chocolate. Yield: 36 servings

Per Serving: Calories 129; Fat 8 g; Sodium 139 mg; Dietary Fiber <1 g

DESSERTS

Rainbow Fruit Cups

½ cup vanilla yogurt
½ cup frozen whipped topping, thawed
2 tablespoons orange juice
1½ teaspoons orange zest
2 (11-ounce) cans mandarin oranges, drained
2 cups juice-pack canned pineapple chunks
2 bananas, sliced
2 red apples, peeled, sliced
1 gallon rainbow sherbet

Mix the yogurt, whipped topping, orange juice and orange zest in a medium mixing bowl. Chill, covered, in the refrigerator. Combine the oranges, undrained pineapple, bananas and apples in a medium mixing bowl and mix gently. Chill, covered, in the refrigerator. Spoon 1 scoop of the sherbet into each of 16 dessert goblets or dessert bowls. Spoon several tablespoons of the fruit mixture over the sherbet. Top with the yogurt mixture. Yield: 16 servings

Per Serving: Calories 353; Fat 5 g; Sodium 99 mg; Dietary Fiber 2 g

Peaches and Cream Cheesecake

¾ cup all-purpose flour
1 (4-ounce) package vanilla instant
    pudding mix
½ teaspoon salt
½ cup milk
1 egg, lightly beaten
3 tablespoons butter or margarine,
    softened
1 (28-ounce) can juice-pack sliced
    peaches
8 ounces cream cheese, softened
½ cup plus 1 tablespoon sugar, divided
½ teaspoon ground cinnamon

Preheat the oven to 350°F. Combine the flour, pudding mix and salt in a medium mixing bowl and mix well. Add the milk, egg and butter, stirring until blended. Pat over the bottom and up the side of a greased 9- or 10-inch round baking dish. Drain the peaches, reserving 3 tablespoons of the juice. Arrange the peach slices over the prepared layer. Beat the cream cheese, ½ cup of the sugar and reserved peach juice in a large mixer bowl until blended, scraping the bowl occasionally. Spread over the peaches. Sprinkle with a mixture of the remaining 1 tablespoon sugar and cinnamon. Bake for 30 minutes or until set. Let stand until cool. Chill, covered, in the refrigerator. Yield: 8 servings

Per Serving: Calories 342; Fat 16 g; Sodium 471 mg; Dietary Fiber 2 g

DESSERTS

Creamy Peach Melba Flans

1 (16-ounce) package pound cake mix
¼ cup orange juice
1 tablespoon orange zest
1½ cups low-fat peach yogurt
½ cup cold skim milk
1 (6-ounce) package vanilla instant
   pudding mix
8 ounces frozen nonfat whipped
   topping, thawed
4 fresh peaches, peeled, sliced
1 cup fresh raspberries
1 cup orange marmalade

Preheat the oven to 350°F. Coat the sides and bottoms of two 10-inch round baking pans lightly with vegetable oil. Line the bottoms with cooking parchment. Prepare the cake mix using package directions, substituting the orange juice for ¼ cup of the liquid. Stir in the orange zest. Spoon the batter into the prepared flan pans. Bake for 20 to 25 minutes or until a wooden pick inserted in the center comes out clean. Cool in the pans on a wire rack for 10 minutes. Invert onto a wire rack. Let stand until cool. Arrange on 2 serving platters. Whisk the yogurt and skim milk in a medium mixing bowl until blended. Add the pudding mix, whisking until smooth. Whisk in the whipped topping. Spread evenly over the baked layers. Arrange the peaches and raspberries over the top in a decorative pattern. Brush the fruit lightly with the orange marmalade. Yield: 16 servings

Per Serving: Calories 298; Fat 8 g; Sodium 282 mg; Dietary Fiber 1 g

COOK'S TIP May substitute two 16-ounce packages frozen peach slices thawed and patted dry for the fresh peaches and/or drained thawed frozen raspberries for the fresh raspberries.

Raspberry Sauce

1 (10-ounce) package frozen raspberries in light syrup, thawed
½ cup raspberry jam
1 teaspoon lemon zest
1 tablespoon fresh lemon juice
1½ teaspoons cornstarch

Combine the raspberries, jam and lemon zest in a 2-quart saucepan. Bring to a boil over low heat, stirring occasionally. Cook for 6 to 8 minutes or until of the desired consistency, stirring constantly. Press the mixture through a sieve, discarding the seeds and zest. Return the mixture to the saucepan. Stir in a mixture of the lemon juice and cornstarch. Cook over low heat until thickened, stirring constantly. Chill, covered, stirring occasionally during the cooling process. Serve over vanilla ice cream, lemon ice cream and/or frozen yogurt. Yield: 8 servings

Per Serving: Calories 72; Fat 0 g; Sodium 10 mg; Dietary Fiber <1 g

DESSERTS

Tortoni Squares

1 cup fine vanilla wafer crumbs
⅓ cup chopped toasted almonds
3 tablespoons melted butter or
   margarine
1 teaspoon almond extract
3 pints vanilla ice cream, softened
1 (12-ounce) jar apricot or peach
   preserves

Mix the vanilla wafer crumbs, almonds, butter and flavoring in a medium mixing bowl. Reserve ¼ cup of the crumb mixture. Layer the remaining crumb mixture, ice cream and preserves ½ at a time in an 8x8-inch dish lined with foil. Sprinkle with the reserved crumbs. Freeze, covered, until set. Cut into 9 squares. Yield: 9 servings

Per Serving: Calories 376; Fat 17 g; Sodium 159 mg; Dietary Fiber 1 g

Five-Minute Devil's Food Cake

1 teaspoon baking soda
½ cup buttermilk
2 cups sifted all-purpose flour
3 tablespoons unsweetened cocoa powder
½ teaspoon salt
3 cups sugar, divided
½ cup plus 1 tablespoon vegetable shortening, divided
2 eggs
1 cup boiling water
1½ teaspoons vanilla extract, divided
1 ounce semiswet chocolate
⅓ cup milk

Preheat the oven to 375°F. Dissolve the baking soda in the buttermilk and mix well. Sift the flour, cocoa powder and salt together. Combine 2 cups of the sugar and ½ cup of the shortening in a large mixer bowl. Beat at high speed until light and fluffy, scraping the bowl occasionally. Add the eggs, beating until blended. Beat in the baking soda mixture. Add the flour mixture and mix well. Stir in the boiling water and 1 teaspoon of the vanilla. Spoon into a greased and lightly floured 9x13-inch cake pan. Bake for 25 to 30 minutes or until a wooden pick inserted in the center comes out clean. Cool in the pan on a wire rack. Bring the remaining 1 cup sugar, remaining 1 tablespoon shortening, remaining ½ teaspoon vanilla, chocolate and milk to a boil in a 2-quart saucepan. Boil for 1 minute, stirring frequently. Remove from heat. Beat for several minutes or until thick and smooth and of spreading consistency. Spread over the cooled cake.

Yield: 15 servings

Per Serving: Calories 309; Fat 10 g; Sodium 177 mg; Dietary Fiber 1 g

DESSERTS

Out-of-this-World Cake

1 (2-layer) package yellow cake mix
1 (20-ounce) can crushed pineapple
3 cups milk
1 (6-ounce) package vanilla instant
    pudding mix
1 teaspoon vanilla extract
8 ounces cream cheese, softened
12 ounces frozen whipped topping,
    thawed
1 cup shredded coconut
1 cup chopped pecans

Prepare and bake the cake using package directions for a 9x13-inch cake pan. Pierce the top of the cake with a fork. Pour the undrained pineapple over the baked layer. Mix the milk, pudding mix and vanilla in a medium mixing bowl. Beat the cream cheese in a medium mixer bowl at high speed until light and fluffy. Add the pudding mixture, beating until smooth. Spread over the prepared layers. Top with the whipped topping. Sprinkle with the coconut and pecans. Chill, covered, for several hours. Yield: 15 servings

Per Serving: Calories 463; Fat 24 g; Sodium 460 mg; Dietary Fiber 2 g

Quick-and-Easy Jam Cake

Cake
1 (2-layer) package spice cake mix
4 eggs
1 cup seedless blackberry jam
⅓ cup vegetable oil
⅔ cup raisins
⅔ cup chopped pecans
Brown Sugar Frosting
1 (1-pound) package confectioners' sugar
¼ cup milk
2 ounces cream cheese, softened
1 cup packed light brown sugar
⅓ cup butter or margarine

Preheat the oven to 350°F. For the cake, combine the cake mix, eggs, jam and oil in a large mixer bowl. Beat at medium-high speed until smooth, scraping the bowl occasionally. Stir in the raisins and pecans. Spoon into 3 greased and floured 9-inch cake pans. Bake for 18 minutes or until a wooden pick inserted in the center comes out clean. Cool in the pans for 10 minutes. Invert onto a wire rack to cool completely. For the frosting, combine the confectioners' sugar, milk and cream cheese in a large mixer bowl. Heat the brown sugar and butter in a small saucepan over medium-low heat until the brown sugar dissolves, stirring frequently. Add to the confectioners' sugar mixture. Beat at medium-high speed until smooth and of spreading consistency. Spread between the layers and over the top and side of the cake. Yield: 16 servings

Per Serving: Calories 510; Fat 18 g; Sodium 334 mg; Dietary Fiber 1 g

DESSERTS

Strawberry Cake

1 (2-layer) package white cake mix
½ cup water
½ cup vegetable oil
3 eggs
1 (3-ounce) package strawberry gelatin dessert
½ cup mashed fresh strawberries
1 tablespoon all-purpose flour
8 ounces frozen whipped topping, thawed
1½ cups sliced fresh strawberries
Sprigs of fresh mint (optional)

Preheat the oven to 350°F. Combine the cake mix, water and oil in a large mixer bowl. Beat until blended. Add the eggs 1 at a time, beating well after each addition. Mix the gelatin, mashed strawberries and flour in a small mixing bowl. Add to the cake mix mixture and mix well. Spoon into a greased and floured 9x13-inch cake pan. Bake for 30 to 35 minutes or until a wooden pick inserted in the center comes out clean. Cool in the pan on a wire rack. Spread with the whipped topping. Serve immediately or store, covered, in the refrigerator until just before serving time. Top each serving with sliced fresh strawberries and mint sprigs just before serving. Yield: 12 servings

Per Serving: Calories 380; Fat 18 g; Sodium 323 mg; Dietary Fiber 1 g

Rocky Road Fudge

2 cups semisweet chocolate morsels
1 (14-ounce) can sweetened condensed
    milk
2 tablespoons butter or margarine
2 cups dry-roasted peanuts
1 (10-ounce) package miniature
    marshmallows

Combine the chocolate morsels, condensed milk and butter in a double boiler. Cook over boiling water until blended, stirring constantly. Remove from heat. Stir the peanuts and marshmallows into the chocolate mixture. Spread the chocolate mixture in a 9x13-inch dish lined with waxed paper. Chill, covered, for 2 hours or until set. Cut into 36 squares. Store, covered, at room temperature. Yield: 36 squares

Per Serving: Calories 161; Fat 8 g; Sodium 25 mg; Dietary Fiber 1 g

DESSERTS

Chocolate Crunch Brownies

2 cups sugar
1 cup butter or margarine, softened
4 eggs
1 cup all-purpose flour
6 tablespoons unsweetened cocoa
   powder
2 teaspoons vanilla extract
½ teaspoon salt
1 (7-ounce) jar marshmallow creme
2 cups semisweet chocolate morsels
1 cup creamy peanut butter
3 cups crisp rice cereal

Preheat the oven to 350°F. Combine the sugar and butter in a large mixer bowl. Beat at high speed until creamy, scraping the bowl occasionally. Add the eggs, beating until blended. Stir in the flour, cocoa powder, vanilla and salt. Spoon into a greased 9x13-inch baking pan. Bake for 25 minutes or until the edges pull from the sides of the pan. Cool in the pan on a wire rack. Spread with the marshmallow creme. Combine the chocolate morsels and peanut butter in a 2-quart saucepan. Cook over low heat until blended, stirring constantly. Remove from heat. Stir in the cereal. Spread over the prepared layers. Chill, covered, until set. Cut into 36 bars. Store, covered, in the refrigerator. Yield: 36 brownies

Per Serving: Calories 226; Fat 12 g; Sodium 153 mg; Dietary Fiber 1 g

Rich Chocolate Mint Brownies

4 ounces unsweetened chocolate,
  divided
½ cup plus 3 tablespoons butter or
  margarine, softened, divided
1 cup sugar
2 eggs, lightly beaten
½ cup all-purpose flour
½ cup coarsely chopped pecans
1 teaspoon peppermint extract, divided
⅛ teaspoon salt
1 cup confectioners' sugar
1 tablespoon half-and-half or
  evaporated milk

Preheat the oven to 350°F. Combine 2 ounces of the chocolate and ½ cup of the butter in a large microwave-safe dish. Microwave on High for 1½ to 2 minutes or until blended, stirring halfway through the cooking process. Cool slightly. Stir in the sugar and eggs. Add the flour, pecans, ¼ teaspoon of the flavoring and salt and mix well. Spoon into a greased 7x11-inch baking pan. Bake for 20 minutes or until a wooden pick inserted in the center comes out clean. Cool in the pan on a wire rack. Mix the confectioners' sugar, half-and-half, 2 tablespoons of the remaining butter and the remaining ¾ teaspoon flavoring in a large mixing bowl until smooth. Spread over the brownie layer. Chill for 30 minutes or until set. Combine the remaining 2 ounces chocolate and remaining 1 tablespoon butter in a small microwave-safe dish. Microwave on High for 1 to 1½ minutes or until blended, stirring halfway through the cooking process. Drizzle over the top, spreading evenly to cover the surface. Chill until set. Cut into 1½-inch squares. Yield: 40 squares

Per Serving: Calories 94; Fat 6 g; Sodium 43 mg; Dietary Fiber 1 g

DESSERTS

Easy Cheesecake Squares

1 cup all-purpose flour
½ cup finely chopped walnuts
⅓ cup packed brown sugar
⅓ cup melted butter or margarine
8 ounces cream cheese, softened
¼ cup sugar
1 egg
2 tablespoons milk
1 tablespoon lemon juice
1 teaspoon vanilla extract

Preheat the oven to 350°F. Mix the flour, walnuts and brown sugar in a medium mixing bowl. Add the butter, stirring until crumbly. Reserve 1 cup of the crumb mixture. Press the remaining crumb mixture over the bottom of a greased 8x8-inch baking pan. Bake for 12 to 15 minutes or until light brown. Beat the cream cheese and sugar in a medium mixer bowl at high speed until light and fluffy. Add the egg, milk, lemon juice and vanilla and mix well. Spread over the baked layer. Sprinkle with the reserved crumb mixture. Bake for 25 minutes. Cool in the pan on a wire rack. Chill before serving. Cut into 2-inch squares. Store, covered, in the refrigerator. Yield: 16 squares

Per Serving: Calories 171; Fat 12 g; Sodium 88 mg; Dietary Fiber <1 g

Coconut Crisps

1½ cups all-purpose flour
1¼ cups old-fashioned oats
¾ cup flaked coconut
1 teaspoon baking powder
½ teaspoon baking soda
½ teaspoon salt
1 cup butter or margarine, softened
1 cup sugar
1 cup packed light brown sugar
1 egg

Preheat the oven to 375°F. Mix the flour, oats, coconut, baking powder, baking soda and salt in a medium mixing bowl. Combine the butter, sugar and brown sugar in a large mixer bowl. Beat at high speed until light and fluffy, scraping the bowl occasionally. Add the egg, beating until blended. Add the flour mixture and mix well. Shape into small balls. Arrange 2 inches apart on an ungreased cookie sheet. Flatten with a fork. Bake for 8 to 10 minutes or until light brown. Cool on the cookie sheet for 2 minutes. Remove to a wire rack to cool completely.
Yield: 60 cookies

Per Serving: Calories 79; Fat 4 g; Sodium 72 mg; Dietary Fiber <1 g

DESSERTS

149

Cookie Kisses

1 (18-ounce) package refrigerated
   chocolate chip cookie dough
36 chocolate candy kisses, unwrapped

Preheat the oven to 350°F. Slice the dough into nine 1-inch-thick slices. Cut each slice into quarters. Place 1 dough quarter in each of 36 miniature muffin cups sprayed with nonstick cooking spray. Press the dough over the bottom and up the side of each muffin cup. Place 1 candy kiss in each prepared muffin cup. Bake for 10 to 12 minutes or until the edges are light brown. Cool in the muffin cups on a wire rack for 15 minutes. Remove to a wire rack to cool completely. Yield: 36 cookies

Per Serving: Calories 87; Fat 4 g; Sodium 34 mg; Dietary Fiber <1 g

Stars Lemon Bars

2 cups all-purpose flour, divided
½ cup plus 3 tablespoons confectioners'
    sugar, divided
¾ cup butter or margarine, chilled, cut
    into pats
3 cups sugar
6 eggs
1 cup plus 2 tablespoons fresh lemon
    juice

Preheat the oven to 325°F. Combine 1½ cups of the flour and ½ cup of the confectioners' sugar in a medium mixing bowl. Cut in the butter until crumbly. Press over the bottom of a 9x13-inch baking pan. Bake for 20 to 25 minutes or until golden brown. Reduce the oven temperature to 300°F. Whisk the sugar and eggs in a medium mixing bowl until blended. Stir in the remaining ½ cup flour and lemon juice. Spread evenly over the baked layer. Bake for 40 minutes longer or until set. Cool in the pan on a wire rack for 30 minutes. Sprinkle with the remaining 3 tablespoons confectioners' sugar. Cut into 20 bars. Yield: 20 bars

Per Serving: Calories 264; Fat 9 g; Sodium 90 mg; Dietary Fiber <1 g

DESSERTS

Pecan Pie Squares

3 cups all-purpose flour
1½ cups plus 6 tablespoons sugar, divided
¾ cup butter or margarine, softened
¾ teaspoon salt
1½ cups light corn syrup
4 eggs, lightly beaten
3 tablespoons melted butter or
    margarine
1½ teaspoons vanilla extract
2½ cups chopped pecans

Preheat the oven to 350°F. Combine the flour, 6 tablespoons of the sugar, ¾ cup butter and salt in a medium mixer bowl. Beat at medium speed until crumbly. Press over the bottom of a greased 10x15-inch baking pan. Bake for 20 minutes or until golden brown. Combine the remaining 1½ cups sugar, corn syrup, eggs, 3 tablespoons melted butter and vanilla in a medium mixer bowl. Beat at medium speed until blended. Stir in the pecans. Spread evenly over the baked layer. Bake for 25 minutes longer or until set. Cool in the pan on a wire rack. Cut into 1½-inch squares. Yield: 70 squares

Per Serving: Calories 114; Fat 6 g; Sodium 62 mg; Dietary Fiber <1 g

Peppermint Candy Cookies

1 cup butter or margarine, softened
1 cup confectioners' sugar, divided
2½ cups all-purpose flour
1 teaspoon vanilla extract
½ cup finely crushed peppermint candy
3 ounces cream cheese, softened
1 teaspoon milk
2 or 3 drops of red food coloring

Preheat the oven to 350°F. Combine the butter and ½ cup of the confectioners' sugar in a medium mixer bowl. Beat at medium-high speed until light and fluffy, scraping the bowl occasionally. Add the flour gradually, beating constantly until blended. Mix in the vanilla. Chill the dough, covered, in the refrigerator. Mix the remaining ½ cup confectioners' sugar and peppermint candy in a medium mixing bowl. Combine the cream cheese, milk and food coloring in a small mixing bowl and mix well. Stir into the candy mixture. Shape the dough into 1-inch balls. Arrange on an ungreased cookie sheet. Make an indentation in the center of each ball with thumb. Spoon ¼ teaspoon of the candy mixture into each indentation. Seal the edges over the filling. Bake for 12 to 15 minutes or until set; do not brown. Cool on the cookie sheet for 2 minutes. Remove to a wire rack to cool completely. Yield: 36 cookies

Per Serving: Calories 109; Fat 6 g; Sodium 60 mg; Dietary Fiber <1 g

DESSERTS

Harvest Pumpkin Bars

2 cups all-purpose flour
2 cups sugar
1 tablespoon pumpkin pie spice
2 teaspoons ground cinnamon
2 teaspoons baking powder
1 teaspoon baking soda
½ teaspoon salt
1 (15-ounce) can solid-pack pumpkin
¾ cup vegetable oil
4 eggs, beaten
3 ounces cream cheese, softened
6 tablespoons butter or margarine, softened
1 teaspoon milk
1 teaspoon vanilla extract
2 cups confectioners' sugar

Preheat the oven to 350°F. Mix the flour, sugar, pumpkin pie spice, cinnamon, baking powder, baking soda and salt in a large mixing bowl. Stir in the pumpkin, oil and eggs. Spread in a greased 10x15-inch baking pan. Bake for 20 to 25 minutes or until the edges pull from the sides of the pan. Cool in the pan on a wire rack. Combine the cream cheese, butter, milk and vanilla in a medium mixer bowl. Beat at medium-high speed until smooth, scraping the bowl occasionally. Add the confectioners' sugar, beating constantly until of spreading consistency. Spread over the baked layer. Chill, covered, until serving time. Cut into 48 bars. Yield: 48 bars

Per Serving: Calories 130; Fat 6 g; Sodium 97 mg; Dietary Fiber 1 g

Freeze for future use if desired.

Caramel Walnut Thumbprint Cookies

4 cups all-purpose flour
1 teaspoon baking soda
½ teaspoon salt
2½ cups packed brown sugar, divided
1 cup butter or margarine, softened
2 eggs
2 teaspoons vanilla extract
½ cup sour cream
2 cups finely chopped walnuts

Preheat the oven to 350°F. Mix the flour, baking soda and salt in a medium mixing bowl. Combine 1½ cups of the brown sugar and butter in a medium mixer bowl. Beat at high speed until light and fluffy. Add the eggs and vanilla. Beat until blended. Add the flour mixture and mix well. Shape the dough into 1-inch balls. Arrange 2 inches apart on an ungreased cookie sheet. Make an indentation in the center of each ball with thumb. Combine the remaining 1 cup brown sugar and sour cream in a medium mixing bowl and mix well. Stir in the walnuts. Spoon 1 teaspoon of the walnut mixture into each indentation. Bake for 12 minutes or until the edges are firm to the touch and golden brown. Cool on the cookie sheet for 2 minutes. Remove to a wire rack to cool completely. Yield: 60 cookies

Per Serving: Calories 124; Fat 6 g; Sodium 79 mg; Dietary Fiber <1 g

DESSERTS

Apricot Pecan Tassies

1 cup all-purpose flour
½ cup butter or margarine, cut into pats
6 tablespoons reduced-fat cream cheese
¾ cup packed light brown sugar
1 egg, lightly beaten
1 tablespoon butter or margarine, softened
½ teaspoon vanilla extract
¼ teaspoon salt
⅔ cup finely chopped dried apricots
⅓ cup chopped pecans

Preheat the oven to 325°F. Combine the flour, ½ cup butter and cream cheese in a blender container or food processor. Process until the mixture forms a ball. Chill, wrapped in plastic wrap, for 15 minutes. Combine the brown sugar, egg, 1 tablespoon butter, vanilla and salt in a medium mixer bowl. Beat at medium-high speed until smooth. Stir in the apricots and pecans. Shape the dough into twenty-four 1-inch balls. Press the balls over the bottoms and up the sides of 24 greased miniature muffin cups. Spoon the apricot mixture into the prepared muffin cups. Bake for 25 minutes or until the filling is set. Cool in the muffin cups on a wire rack. Yield: 24 tassies

Per Serving: Calories 115; Fat 6 g; Sodium 93 mg; Dietary Fiber 1 g

Crustless Apple Pie

¾ cup sugar
½ cup all-purpose flour
1 teaspoon baking powder
¼ teaspoon salt
1 egg, lightly beaten
1 teaspoon vanilla extract
2 cups sliced tart apples
½ cup chopped pecans

Preheat the oven to 350°F. Combine the sugar, flour, baking powder and salt in a medium mixing bowl and mix well. Stir in the egg and vanilla. Add the apples and pecans, stirring until mixed. Spoon into a buttered 10-inch deep-dish pie plate. Bake for 30 minutes or until the apples are tender. Serve with whipped cream, whipped topping or ice cream. Yield: 6 servings

Per Serving: Calories 235; Fat 8 g; Sodium 189 mg; Dietary Fiber 2 g

DESSERTS

Chocolate Truffle Tart

¾ cup whipping cream
⅓ cup milk
8 ounces semisweet chocolate, chopped
1 egg, lightly beaten
1 baked (9-inch) tart shell or pie shell
   Whipped cream (optional)

Preheat the oven to 350°F. Combine the whipping cream and milk in a heavy 2-quart saucepan. Cook over medium heat until hot, stirring occasionally. Remove from heat. Add the chocolate, stirring until blended. Let stand for 5 minutes. Whisk in the egg. Spoon the chocolate mixture into the baked tart or pie shell. Bake for 20 to 25 minutes or until the filling is set and firm to the touch. Cool on a wire rack. Serve at room temperature for a soft, custardy texture or serve chilled for a fudgy texture. Garnish with whipped cream. Yield: 8 servings

Per Serving: Calories 309; Fat 26 g; Sodium 124 mg; Dietary Fiber 1 g

Kiwi Lime Pie

¾ cup sugar
⅓ cup all-purpose flour
⅛ teaspoon salt
1¾ cups milk
3 eggs, beaten
¼ cup butter or margarine
¼ cup lime juice
2 teaspoons lime zest
1 cup lemon yogurt
  Green food coloring
1 baked (9-inch) pie shell, cooled
¼ cup apple jelly
1 cup whipped cream
2 or 3 kiwifruit, sliced
1 or 2 limes, sliced

Mix the sugar, flour and salt in a 2-quart saucepan. Whisk the milk in gradually. Cook over medium heat until thick and bubbly, stirring constantly. Reduce heat to low. Cook for 2 minutes longer, stirring constantly. Remove from heat. Stir 1 cup of the hot mixture into the eggs; stir the eggs into the hot mixture. Cook over medium-low heat until thickened, stirring constantly; do not boil. Remove from heat. Stir in the butter, lime juice and lime zest. Fold in the yogurt. Add the desired amount of food coloring and mix well. Let stand, covered with plastic wrap, until cool. Brush the baked pie shell with the apple jelly. Spoon the lime mixture into the pie shell. Chill, covered, for 8 to 10 hours. Spoon the whipped cream into a pastry bag. Pipe the whipped cream around the outer edge of the pie. Alternate the kiwifruit slices and lime slices in a decorative pattern on the whipped cream. Yield: 8 servings

Per Serving: Calories 421; Fat 21 g; Sodium 279 mg; Dietary Fiber 2 g

DESSERTS

Sweet Potato Pie

1½ cups mashed cooked sweet potatoes
1 cup milk
½ cup sugar
3 eggs, lightly beaten
2 tablespoons melted butter or
    margarine
1 teaspoon allspice
1 teaspoon ground cinnamon
1 unbaked (9-inch) pie shell

Preheat the oven to 350°F. Combine the sweet potatoes, milk, sugar, eggs, butter, allspice and cinnamon in a medium mixing bowl and mix well. Spoon into the pie shell. Bake for 40 to 45 minutes or until set. Cool on a wire rack before serving. Yield: 6 servings

Per Serving: Calories 355; Fat 15 g; Sodium 237 mg; Dietary Fiber 2 g

Apple Dessert Pizza

2 cups all-purpose flour
½ cup plus 2 tablespoons sugar, divided
½ teaspoon baking powder
¼ teaspoon salt
½ cup 70% vegetable oil spread
1 egg
1 tablespoon water
1 teaspoon ground cinnamon
4 medium Granny Smith apples, peeled,
  thinly sliced
½ cup apricot preserves

Preheat the oven to 350°F. Combine the flour, ½ cup of the sugar, baking powder and salt in a large mixing bowl and mix well. Cut in the vegetable oil spread until crumbly. Whisk the egg and water in a small bowl until blended. Add to the flour mixture, stirring until the mixture forms a ball. Pat the dough over the bottom and up the side of a 14-inch pizza pan. Sprinkle with a mixture of the remaining 2 tablespoons sugar and cinnamon. Arrange the apple slices in concentric circles over the dough, beginning at the outside edge and overlapping slightly. Fill the center with the remaining slices to form a blossom shape. Bake for 40 minutes or until the apples are tender and the crust is light golden brown. Remove to a cooling rack. Spoon the preserves into a microwave-safe dish. Microwave on High for 30 to 45 seconds or until melted. Brush the preserves over the warm pizza. Cut into wedges. Serve warm or cool. Yield: 10 servings

Per Serving: Calories 287; Fat 9 g; Sodium 184 mg; Dietary Fiber 2 g

The 70% vegetable oil spread is a reduced-fat product available in sticks in the dairy section of the grocery store. For best results, do not use tub, soft or whipped products for baking. The added water and air in these products can cause baked goods to be thin, flat and tough.

DESSERTS

Chocolate Pizza

2 cups semisweet chocolate morsels
16 ounces white almond bark, divided
1 cup crisp rice cereal
1 cup peanuts
2 cups miniature marshmallows
1 (6-ounce) jar red maraschino cherries, drained, cut into halves
2 tablespoons drained green maraschino cherry quarters
½ cup shredded coconut
1 teaspoon vegetable oil

Combine the chocolate morsels and 14 ounces of the almond bark in a heavy 2-quart saucepan. Cook over low heat until smooth, stirring constantly. Remove from heat. Add the cereal and peanuts and mix well. Stir in the marshmallows. Spread in a greased 12-inch pizza pan. Top with the cherries. Sprinkle with the coconut. Combine the remaining 2 ounces almond bark and oil in a 1-quart saucepan. Cook over low heat until smooth, stirring constantly. Drizzle over the chocolate mixture. Chill, covered, until set. Store at room temperature.

Yield: 20 servings

Per Serving: Calories 293; Fat 17 g; Sodium 47 mg; Dietary Fiber 1 g

SPECIAL OCCASIONS

From tender roasts to luscious desserts, here are the favorite foods families anticipate on special occasions, plus menus built around these recipes to help you create memorable, new traditions—especially at holiday times.

MENU

NEW YEAR'S EVE

Gather friends together to ring in the New Year with an elegant yet easy dinner party.

North Stars   p.166
Seafood Primavera Squares   p.11
Spinach Salad with Vinaigrette Dressing
Oriental Pork Tenderloin   p.167
Gingery Rice Pilaf   p.124
Vanilla Ice Cream or Frozen Yogurt with Raspberry Sauce   p.139
Mock Champagne   p.168

North Stars

1 (11-ounce) package refrigerated
   French bread dough
1 cup shredded Swiss cheese
½ cup mayonnaise
½ cup sour cream
1 envelope Italian salad dressing mix
½ cup chopped red bell pepper
½ cup chopped green bell pepper

Preheat the oven to 375°F. Bake the bread dough using package directions. Let stand until cool. Cut the loaf into twenty-four ¼-inch slices with a serrated knife. Arrange the slices cut side up on an 11x17-inch baking sheet. Combine the cheese, mayonnaise, sour cream and dressing mix in a medium mixing bowl and mix well. Spread some of the cheese mixture on each slice. Sprinkle with the bell peppers. Bake for 10 to 12 minutes or until bubbly. Yield: 24 slices

Per Serving: Calories 92; Fat 6 g; Sodium 217 mg; Dietary Fiber <1 g

Oriental Pork Tenderloin

½ cup soy sauce
6 tablespoons rice vinegar
¼ cup chopped green onions
6 garlic cloves, pressed
2 teaspoons minced fresh ginger root
1 teaspoon red pepper flakes
3 pounds pork tenderloin
1 cup cold water
4 teaspoons cornstarch

Combine the soy sauce, rice vinegar, green onions, garlic, ginger root and red pepper flakes in a 2-gallon sealable plastic bag. Add the pork and seal tightly. Turn the bag to coat the pork. Marinate in the refrigerator for 30 minutes, turning several times. Drain, reserving the marinade. Preheat the oven to 425°F. Arrange the pork in a roasting pan. Bake, uncovered, for 30 to 40 minutes or until a meat thermometer registers 160°F. Let stand, loosely covered with foil, for 10 minutes. Bring the reserved marinade to a boil in a 1-quart saucepan. Stir in a mixture of the cold water and cornstarch. Bring to a boil. Boil for 2 minutes, stirring occasionally. Cut the pork into ½-inch slices. Serve with the sauce. Yield: 10 servings

Per Serving: Calories 184; Fat 5 g; Sodium 1110 mg; Dietary Fiber <1 g

SPECIAL OCCASIONS

Mock Champagne

4 cups white grape juice, chilled
4 cups ginger ale, chilled
Crushed ice

Combine the grape juice and ginger ale in a pitcher and mix well. Pour over crushed ice in tall slender glasses immediately. Yield: 8 servings (8 cups)

Per Serving: Calories 115; Fat <1 g; Sodium 16 mg; Dietary Fiber <1 g

MENU

VALENTINE'S DAY

Light the candles and treat yourselves to an intimate dinner for two.

Crostini with Sun-Dried Tomatoes   p.9
Winter Fruit Salad with Honey Lime Dressing   p.103
Steak Diane   p.170
Classic Risotto   p.125
Creamy Spinach and Artichokes   p.171
Chocolate Lover's Cheesecake   p.172

Steak Diane

2 tablespoons butter or margarine
1 tablespoon minced shallot
1 cup sliced mushrooms
2 (6-ounce) beef tenderloin steaks
  Salt and pepper to taste
¼ cup beef broth
2 tablespoons apple juice
2½ teaspoons Dijon mustard
1 teaspoon Worcestershire sauce

Heat the butter in a 10-inch skillet over medium heat until melted. Add the shallot and mix well. Cook for 1 minute. Stir in the mushrooms. Cook for 3 to 4 minutes or until tender, stirring constantly. Remove the mushroom mixture to a bowl with a slotted spoon, reserving the pan drippings. Sprinkle both sides of the steaks with salt and pepper. Cook the steaks in the reserved pan drippings over medium-high heat for 10 to 12 minutes for medium or until of the desired degree of doneness, turning once. Remove the steaks to a platter. Cover to keep warm. Pour a mixture of the broth, apple juice, Dijon mustard and Worcestershire sauce into the same skillet. Stir in the mushroom mixture. Bring to a boil. Cook for 1 minute or until slightly reduced and of a sauce consistency, stirring constantly. Spoon the mushroom sauce over the steaks. Yield: 2 servings

Per Serving: Calories 393; Fat 24 g; Sodium 482 mg; Dietary Fiber 1 g

Creamy Spinach and Artichokes

1 (14-ounce) can artichoke hearts,
   drained
1 (9-ounce) package frozen creamed
   spinach, thawed
2 tablespoons Italian bread crumbs
2 tablespoons grated Parmesan cheese
2 teaspoons olive oil

Preheat the oven to 350°F. Cut the artichoke hearts into halves. Arrange in a greased 8x8-inch baking dish. Spoon the spinach over the artichokes. Mix the bread crumbs and cheese in a small bowl. Sprinkle over the spinach. Drizzle with the olive oil. Bake for 20 minutes or until heated through. Yield: 3 servings

Per Serving: Calories 225; Fat 14 g; Sodium 1148 mg; Dietary Fiber <1 g

SPECIAL OCCASIONS

Chocolate Lover's Cheesecake

1½ cups miniature semisweet chocolate
  morsels
8 ounces cream cheese, softened
¼ cup butter or margarine, softened
⅓ cup sugar
¾ cup chopped pecans
1½ teaspoons vanilla extract
1 cup whipping cream, whipped
⅓ cup chocolate syrup, divided
  Sweetened whipped cream (optional)

Line a 5-cup heart-shape mold with foil. Heat the chocolate morsels in a double boiler over hot water until melted, stirring frequently. Combine the cream cheese, butter and sugar in a medium mixer bowl. Beat at medium-high speed until light and fluffy, scraping the bowl occasionally. Stir in the melted chocolate, pecans and vanilla. Fold in the whipped cream. Spoon into the prepared mold. Chill, covered, until set. Drizzle a dessert platter with some of the chocolate syrup. Unmold the cheesecake and arrange over the chocolate syrup. Drizzle with the remaining chocolate syrup. Garnish with sweetened whipped cream. Yield: 8 servings

Per Serving: Calories 554; Fat 44 g; Sodium 160 mg; Dietary Fiber 1 g

May subtitute four 1-cup molds for the heart mold.

MENU

SAINT PATRICK'S DAY DINNER

With a little Celtic music, a little wearin' o' the green, and a lot of eatin' o' the buffet, this menu is for the bit o' Irish in us all.

Lucky Leek Soup   p.174

Spinach and Rice Soup   p.175

Fresh Parsnip Slaw   p.176

Corned Beef Dinner   p.177

Soda Bread Muffins   p.178

Rich Chocolate Mint Brownies   p.147

Coffee Mocha Punch   p.40

Lucky Leek Soup

3 cups chopped leeks
4 cups chopped peeled potatoes
3 cups milk
Salt and pepper to taste
½ cup all-purpose flour
¼ cup melted butter or margarine
6 slices crisp-fried bacon, crumbled
½ cup shredded cheddar cheese
¼ cup chopped fresh parsley

Blanch the leeks in boiling water in a 4-quart saucepan; drain. Return the leeks to the pan. Stir in the potatoes, milk, salt and pepper. Cook over medium heat until the vegetables are tender, stirring occasionally. Drain, reserving the liquid and vegetables separately. Mix the flour and butter in the same saucepan. Add the reserved liquid gradually, stirring constantly until blended. Cook over medium heat until thickened, stirring constantly. Add the leek mixture and mix well. Cook just until heated through, stirring frequently. Ladle into soup bowls. Sprinkle with the bacon, cheese and parsley. Yield: 4 servings

Per Serving: Calories 543; Fat 28 g; Sodium 471 mg; Dietary Fiber 4 g

Spinach and Rice Soup

6 cups chicken broth
1 (10-ounce) can cream of celery soup
¾ soup can milk
2 tablespoons parsley flakes
1 tablespoon dried onion flakes
½ teaspoon pepper
2 cups instant rice
1 (10-ounce) package frozen chopped
    spinach, thawed, drained

Combine the broth, soup, milk, parsley flakes, onion flakes and pepper in a 4-quart saucepan and mix well. Stir in the rice and spinach. Bring to a simmer, stirring occasionally. Simmer, covered, for 5 minutes or until the rice is tender, stirring occasionally. Ladle into soup bowls. Yield: 10 servings

Per Serving: Calories 140; Fat 3 g; Sodium 731 mg; Dietary Fiber 1 g

SPECIAL OCCASIONS

Fresh Parsnip Slaw

½ cup sour cream
2 tablespoons finely chopped onion
2 tablespoons finely chopped fresh
   parsley
1 tablespoon fresh lemon juice
1 teaspoon sugar
½ teaspoon salt
⅛ teaspoon pepper
6 medium parsnips, peeled, coarsely
   shredded
2 unpeeled medium apples, finely
   chopped

Combine the sour cream, onion, parsley, lemon juice, sugar, salt and pepper in a large mixing bowl and mix well. Add the parsnips and apples, stirring to coat. Chill, covered, for several hours. Yield: 6 servings

Per Serving: Calories 203; Fat 5 g; Sodium 221 mg; Dietary Fiber 8 g

Corned Beef Dinner

1 (3-pound) corned beef
6 carrots, cut into quarters
6 potatoes, peeled, cut into quarters
1 turnip, peeled, cut into halves
1 large head cabbage, cored, cut into
    quarters

Combine the corned beef with enough water to cover in a stockpot. Bring to a boil. Boil for 2 to 3 hours or until tender, adding additional water as needed. Add the carrots, potatoes and turnip. Boil just until the vegetables are tender, stirring occasionally. Layer the cabbage over the vegetable mixture. Boil for 20 minutes longer. Yield: 6 servings

Per Serving: Calories 516; Fat 26 g; Sodium 1598 mg; Dietary Fiber 10 g

SPECIAL OCCASIONS

Soda Bread Muffins

1½ cups whole wheat flour
½ cup sugar
1 teaspoon baking soda
½ teaspoon salt
1 cup buttermilk

Preheat the oven to 400°F. Combine the whole wheat flour, sugar, baking soda and salt in a medium mixing bowl and mix well. Add the buttermilk, stirring just until moistened. Spoon the batter into 12 greased muffin cups. Bake for 20 minutes. Yield: 12 muffins

Per Serving: Calories 91; Fat <1 g; Sodium 224 mg; Dietary Fiber 2 g

MENU

EASTER BUFFET

Bright springtime flavors make this meal versatile enough to serve for a midmorning brunch or a dinner buffet.

Spinach and Raspberry Salad p.106
Sweet-and-Spicy Ham p.180
Potatoes Anna p.181
Quick Saucy Peas p.115
Dinner Rolls
Out-of-this-World Cake p.142
Kiwi Lime Pie p.159

Sweet-and-Spicy Ham

1 (4- to 5-pound) cooked lean boneless
   ham
2 cups pineapple juice
½ cup packed light brown sugar
1 teaspoon ground cinnamon
½ teaspoon ground ginger
¼ teaspoon ground cloves

Preheat the oven to 350°F. Arrange the ham in a shallow baking pan. Score the top in a diamond pattern. Combine the pineapple juice, brown sugar, cinnamon, ginger and cloves in a 2-quart heavy saucepan and mix well. Bring to a simmer. Simmer for 6 to 8 minutes or until thickened, stirring occasionally. Brush the pineapple sauce over the ham. Bake for 1 to 1½ hours or until a meat thermometer registers 130 degrees, basting frequently with the pineapple sauce. Reheat any remaining sauce and serve with the ham. Yield: 12 servings

Per Serving: Calories 355; Fat 10 g; Sodium 2512 mg; Dietary Fiber <1 g

Potatoes Anna

½ cup melted butter or margarine
6 large baking potatoes (about
    4 pounds)
   Salt and ground pepper to taste

Preheat the oven to 425°F. Brush the bottom and sides of a 1½-quart baking dish generously with some of the butter. Peel and thinly slice the potatoes. Arrange some of the potato slices in a single layer over the bottom of the prepared dish, overlapping the slices slightly. Brush with the butter and sprinkle with salt and pepper. Repeat the layering process with the remaining potatoes and butter until all the ingredients are used, seasoning each layer with salt and pepper. Bake, covered, for 15 minutes. Reduce the oven temperature to 350°F. Bake for 1¼ hours or until the potatoes are tender. Remove the cover. Bake for 5 to 10 minutes longer or until crisp and golden brown. Cool in dish on a wire rack for 5 minutes. Run a metal spatula around the outer edge of the dish and invert the potatoes onto a serving platter if desired. Yield: 6 servings

Per Serving: Calories 281; Fat 16 g; Sodium 167 mg; Dietary Fiber 3 g

SPECIAL OCCASIONS

MENU

MOTHER'S DAY

Go beyond just toast in bed for mom, because she deserves it
more than you'll ever know.

Minty Fruit Bowl   p.183

Cheesy Scrambled Eggs in a Puff   p.184

Swiss Cheese Scramble   p.80

Praline Biscuits   p.86

Berry Whirl   p.185

Coffee or Hot Tea

Minty Fruit Bowl

1 medium honeydew melon, cut into bite-size pieces
2 kiwifruit, cut into quarters, sliced
2 cups seedless green grapes
1 unpeeled Granny Smith apple, cut into bite-size pieces
½ cup minced fresh mint
½ cup fresh lime juice
½ cup fresh lemon juice
3 tablespoons sugar
1 pint blackberries, strawberries or raspberries
2 sprigs of fresh mint (optional)

Toss the melon, kiwifruit, grapes and apple gently in a large serving bowl. Add the minced mint, lime juice, lemon juice and sugar and mix gently. Taste and adjust for sweetness. Chill, covered, for 2 to 3 hours. Let stand at room temperature for 30 minutes before serving. Add the berries, tossing to mix. Garnish with the sprigs of fresh mint. Yield: 10 servings

Per Serving: Calories 124; Fat <1 g; Sodium 37 mg; Dietary Fiber 4 g

SPECIAL OCCASIONS

Cheesy Scrambled Eggs in a Puff

½ cup water
¼ cup butter or margarine
½ cup pancake mix
2 eggs
8 eggs, beaten
1½ cups shredded cheddar cheese
¼ cup chopped green onions
¼ cup chopped green bell pepper
3 tablespoons chopped pimento
¼ teaspoon salt
   Hot pepper sauce to taste
3 tablespoons melted butter or
   margarine

Preheat the oven to 400°F. Combine the water and ¼ cup butter in a 2-quart saucepan. Bring to a boil, stirring occasionally. Add the pancake mix, stirring until the mixture forms a ball. Remove from heat. Add 2 eggs 1 at a time, beating well after each addition. Spread the mixture evenly in a greased 9- or 10-inch round baking dish. Bake for 15 to 18 minutes or until puffed and golden brown. Combine the 8 beaten eggs, cheese, green onions, green pepper, pimento, salt and hot pepper sauce in a medium mixing bowl and mix well. Scramble the egg mixture in 3 tablespoons butter in a 10- or 12-inch skillet over low heat. Spread over the baked layer. Cut into 6 wedges. Yield: 6 servings

Per Serving: Calories 402; Fat 32 g; Sodium 647 mg; Dietary Fiber 1 g

Berry Whirl

1 cup fresh strawberry halves
1 cup fresh pineapple chunks
½ cup fresh raspberries
2 tablespoons thawed frozen limeade
    concentrate

Combine the strawberries, pineapple, raspberries and limeade concentrate in a blender container or food processor. Process until smooth. Pour into 2 goblets. Serve immediately. Yield: 2 servings

Per Serving: Calories 110; Fat 1 g; Sodium 2 mg; Dietary Fiber 5 g

SPECIAL OCCASIONS

MENU

FATHER'S DAY

Dad gets to eat what he wants today, and everyone else likes it too.

Harvest Popcorn   p.32
Tossed Garden Salad
Stuffed Grilled Pork Chops   p.187
Blue Cheese Potatoes   p.116
Apple Cranberry Cookie Cobbler   p.188
Stars Lemon Bars   p.151

Stuffed Grilled Pork Chops

⅓ cup water
1 tablespoon butter or margarine
1 cup herb stuffing mix
½ unpeeled small apple, chopped
¼ small onion, chopped
2 tablespoons chopped walnuts
4 (6-ounce) pork chops, 1 to 1½ inches
    thick

Preheat the grill. Combine the water and butter in a large microwave-safe dish. Microwave on High until the butter melts and stir. Stir in the stuffing mix, apple, onion and walnuts. Cut a horizontal slit into but not through the side of each pork chop to form a pocket or request your butcher to perform this task. Spoon about ¼ cup of the stuffing mixture into each pocket. Grill the pork chops over medium-hot coals for 10 minutes; turn. Grill for 10 to 15 minutes longer or until a meat thermometer registers 160°F. Yield: 4 servings

Per Serving: Calories 320; Fat 11 g; Sodium 719 mg; Dietary Fiber 2 g

 Substitute cod fillets for the pork chops. Prepare as directed above. Grill for 5 minutes. Turn and sprinkle with dill weed. Grill for 5 minutes longer or until the fish flakes easily.

SPECIAL OCCASIONS

Apple Cranberry Cookie Cobbler

1 (16-ounce) can whole cranberry sauce
⅓ cup packed brown sugar
3 tablespoons all-purpose flour
1 teaspoon ground cinnamon
4 Granny Smith apples, peeled, sliced, cut into halves
½ (18-ounce) package refrigerated sugar cookie dough

Preheat the oven to 400°F. Combine the cranberry sauce, brown sugar, flour and cinnamon in a large mixing bowl and mix well. Add the apples, tossing to mix. Spread evenly in a 9x13-inch baking dish. Slice the cookie dough into ¼-inch slices. Arrange evenly over the cranberry mixture. Bake for 30 to 35 minutes or until the apples are tender and the top is golden brown. Yield: 10 servings

Per Serving: Calories 226; Fat 4 g; Sodium 103 mg; Dietary Fiber 2 g

MENU

4TH OF JULY POTLUCK

The best of the season's produce is transformed into casual, crowd-pleasing dishes.

Summer Garden Dip   p.190
Melon Salad with Orange Lime Dressing   p.191
Nutty Pineapple Slaw   p.107
Roasted Tri-Color Pepper Salad   p.108
Peppery Barbecued Ribs   p.192
Hawaiian Turkey Burgers   p.193
Fresh Corn on the Cob
Stars and Stripes Dessert Pizza   p.194

Summer Garden Dip

1   cup sour cream
¼   cup mayonnaise
2   teaspoons sugar
½   teaspoon salt
¼   teaspoon white pepper
1   garlic clove, pressed
¼   cup minced green bell pepper
¼   cup minced green onions
¼   cup minced cucumber, drained
¼   cup minced radishes
¼   cup minced celery

Combine the sour cream, mayonnaise, sugar, salt, white pepper and garlic in a medium mixing bowl and mix well. Stir in the green pepper, green onions, cucumber, radishes and celery. Spoon into a medium serving bowl. Serve with fresh vegetable chunks and/or assorted party crackers. Store, covered, in the refrigerator. Yield: 20 servings

Per Serving: Calories 48; Fat 5 g; Sodium 81 mg; Dietary Fiber <1 g

Melon Salad with Orange Lime Dressing

1 cantaloupe, chilled, cut into ¾-inch
   pieces
1 honeydew melon, chilled, cut into
   ¾-inch pieces
2 cups seedless red grapes, chilled
6 tablespoons fresh lime juice
¼ cup frozen orange juice concentrate
2 teaspoons lime zest
½ teaspoon vanilla extract

Toss the cantaloupe, honeydew melon and grapes in a medium mixing bowl. Mix the lime juice, orange juice concentrate, lime zest and vanilla in a small mixing bowl. Drizzle over the fruit and toss gently to coat. Spoon into a salad bowl.
Yield: 8 servings

Per Serving: Calories 133; Fat <1 g; Sodium 57 mg; Dietary Fiber 2 g

SPECIAL OCCASIONS

Peppery Barbecued Ribs

4 pounds pork spareribs, cut into 2-rib
    pieces
2 cups water
4 teaspoons Worcestershire sauce
2 teaspoons onion powder
1 teaspoon ground red pepper
½ teaspoon garlic powder
⅛ teaspoon black pepper
    Salt to taste
1 cup fresh lemon juice
⅓ cup sugar

Preheat the oven to 400°F. Arrange the spareribs in a single layer on a rack in a shallow roasting pan. Bake for 30 minutes, turning once; drain. Preheat the grill. Combine the water, Worcestershire sauce, onion powder, red pepper, garlic powder, black pepper and salt in a small 2-quart saucepan and mix well. Bring to a boil; reduce heat. Simmer, covered, for 5 minutes. Remove from heat. Stir in the lemon juice and sugar. Arrange the ribs on a grill rack 4 inches above the hot coals. Brush the ribs with half the sauce. Grill for 10 minutes; turn. Brush the ribs with the remaining sauce. Grill for 10 minutes longer or until the ribs are glazed and cooked through. Yield: 4 servings

Per Serving: Calories 932; Fat 65 g; Sodium 255 mg; Dietary Fiber <1 g

Hawaiian Turkey Burgers

1 (8-ounce) can juice-pack pineapple
    slices
1 pound ground turkey
½ cup thinly sliced green onions
½ cup finely chopped red or green bell
    pepper
½ cup dry bread crumbs
1 teaspoon finely chopped ginger root
½ teaspoon salt
1 cup teriyaki sauce
4 hamburger buns

Preheat the grill. Drain the pineapple, reserving ¼ cup of the juice. Combine the reserved juice, ground turkey, green onions, red pepper, bread crumbs, ginger root and salt in a large mixing bowl and mix gently. Shape into four ½-inch-thick patties. Grill the patties over medium-hot coals for 10 to 12 minutes or until the turkey is no longer pink and a meat thermometer registers 165°F, turning once and basting with the teriyaki sauce 2 minutes before the end of the grilling process. Grill the pineapple slices for 5 minutes, basting with the teriyaki sauce. Grill the buns just until warm. Arrange 1 turkey burger on the bottom half of each bun. Top with pineapple slices and the remaining bun half. Yield: 4 servings

Per Serving: Calories 469; Fat 14 g; Sodium 3497 mg; Dietary Fiber 3 g

To broil, arrange the turkey burgers on a broiler rack sprayed with nonstick cooking spray. Broil 4 to 6 inches from the heat source for 10 to 12 minutes or until the turkey is no longer pink, turning once. Baste with the teriyaki sauce before turning the turkey burgers and baste the top after removing the burgers from the oven.

SPECIAL OCCASIONS

Stars and Stripes Dessert Pizza

1½ (8-count) cans refrigerated crescent
    rolls
8 ounces cream cheese, softened
1 cup confectioners' sugar
1 teaspoon lemon juice
1 teaspoon lemon zest
2 medium bananas, sliced
½ cup lemon-lime soda or lemon juice
1 cup fresh blueberries
2 pints fresh strawberries, sliced

Preheat the oven to 350°F. Unroll the crescent roll dough into 3 long strips. Arrange the dough on a 12x15-inch baking sheet, pinching the seams to seal. Bake for 12 to 15 minutes or until golden brown. Cool on the baking sheet on a wire rack. Combine the cream cheese, confectioners' sugar, lemon juice and lemon zest in a medium mixer bowl. Beat at medium speed until light and fluffy, scraping the bowl occasionally. Spread over the baked crust. Dip the banana slices in the lemon-lime soda to prevent browning. Arrange the blueberries in a square in the upper left corner of the baked crust to represent the stars. Alternate rows of strawberries and bananas to represent the stripes. Chill, covered with plastic wrap, for up to 6 hours. Cut into squares just before serving. Yield: 16 servings

Per Serving: Calories 188; Fat 9 g; Sodium 206 mg; Dietary Fiber 2 g

MENU

PUMPKIN CARVING

Kids and adults alike will have fun dining by the flickering glow
of freshly carved pumpkins.

Hot Cheesy Salsa Dip   p.196
Homemade Tortilla Chips   p.196
Chunky Beef Chili   p.197
Pizza Breadsticks   p.13
Cat Cupcakes   p.198
Candy Apple Delight   p.199
Hot Apple Cider

Hot Cheesy Salsa Dip

8 ounces process cheese spread loaf, cubed
3 ounces cream cheese, cubed
1 cup prepared thick and chunky salsa
¼ cup chopped pitted ripe olives

Combine the cheese spread, cream cheese, salsa and ripe olives in a 1-quart microwave-safe bowl. Microwave on High for 2 minutes and stir. Microwave for 1 to 1½ minutes longer or until the dip is bubbly around the edge and the cheese is melted when stirred. Serve with Homemade Tortilla Chips. Yield: 16 servings (2 cups)

Per Serving: Calories 67; Fat 5 g; Sodium 335 mg; Dietary Fiber <1 g

COOK'S TIP To prepare in the oven, bake in an ovenproof baking dish at 350°F for 20 minutes. Remove from oven. Stir until the cheese melts.

Homemade Tortilla Chips

8 (7- or 8-inch) flour tortillas

Preheat the oven to 400°F. Cut each tortilla into 8 wedges with a pizza cutter. Arrange the wedges in batches in a single layer on an 11x17-inch baking sheet. Bake for 6 to 8 minutes or until light brown. Remove the chips to a wire rack to cool. Yield: 16 servings (64 chips)

Per Serving: Calories 80; Fat 2 g; Sodium 117 mg; Dietary Fiber 1 g

Chunky Beef Chili

2 tablespoons vegetable oil, divided
2 pounds beef chuck, cut into ½-inch
    pieces, divided
2 large onions, chopped
2 ribs celery, chopped
2 garlic cloves, pressed
1 (28-ounce) can diced tomatoes
2 cups water
1 tablespoon ground cumin
1 tablespoon dried oregano
1 tablespoon chili powder
½ teaspoon salt
¼ teaspoon ground red pepper
¼ teaspoon ground black pepper

Heat 1 tablespoon of the oil in a 6-quart Dutch oven over medium heat. Add half the beef. Cook for 8 minutes or until brown on all sides, stirring occasionally. Remove the beef to a bowl with a slotted spoon, reserving the pan drippings. Stir the remaining 1 tablespoon oil into the reserved pan drippings. Heat until hot. Add the remaining beef. Cook until brown on all sides, stirring occasionally. Remove the beef to the bowl with a slotted spoon, reserving the pan drippings. Stir the onions, celery and garlic into the pan drippings. Cook over low heat for 5 minutes, stirring frequently. Return the beef to the Dutch oven. Stir in the undrained tomatoes, water, cumin, oregano, chili powder, salt, red pepper and black pepper. Bring to a boil; reduce heat. Simmer over low heat for 2 to 3 hours or until the beef is tender, stirring occasionally. Add additional water ½ cup at a time if needed for the desired consistency. Yield: 8 servings

Per Serving: Calories 238; Fat 10 g; Sodium 386 mg; Dietary Fiber 2 g

SPECIAL OCCASIONS

Cat Cupcakes

1 (2-layer) package any flavor cake mix
3 cups prepared chocolate frosting
9 ounces small jelly beans or
  chocolate-covered raisins
60 (3-inch pieces) black or purple string
  or pull-apart licorice

Preheat the oven to 350°F. Prepare the cake mix using package directions. Fill miniature muffin cups sprayed with nonstick cooking spray ⅔ full. Bake for 13 to 15 minutes or until a wooden pick inserted in the center comes out clean. Cool in muffin cups on a wire rack for 15 minutes. Transfer the cupcakes to a wire rack to cool completely. Spread the top of each cupcake with a small amount of the frosting. Use whole jelly beans to make ears for each cat. Cut the remaining jelly beans into halves and place over the frosting to represent the eyes and noses. Press the licorice pieces under the noses to make whiskers. Yield: 60 cupcakes

Per Serving: Calories 108; Fat 3 g; Sodium 88 mg; Dietary Fiber <1 g

Candy Apple Delight

2 (8-ounce) cans crushed pineapple,
  drained
8 ounces frozen whipped topping,
  thawed
3 Granny Smith apples, peeled, sliced,
  cut into quarters
3 (2-ounce) Snickers candy bars,
  chopped
½ cup peanuts, chopped

Mix the pineapple and whipped topping in a medium mixing bowl. Fold in the apples, candy and peanuts. Chill, covered, until serving time. Yield: 8 servings

Per Serving: Calories 299; Fat 15 g; Sodium 58 mg; Dietary Fiber 3 g

SPECIAL OCCASIONS

MENU

THANKSGIVING FEAST

When it comes to traditions, every family takes the best of the previous generation and combines those traditions with its own. This menu provides a few new twists to traditional holiday fare.

Relish Tray
Wild Rice and Cranberry Salad   p.114
Turkey Breast with Garlic-Roasted Potatoes   p.201
Harvest Stuffing   p.203
Broccoli with Lemon Sauce   p.202
Magical Biscuits   p.85
Sweet Potato Pie   p.160
Pumpkin Cheesecake   p.204

Turkey Breast with Garlic-Roasted Potatoes

1 (3-pound) turkey breast
8 small red potatoes, cut into halves
½ cup chicken broth
2 garlic cloves, pressed
1 teaspoon salt-free seasoning blend

Preheat the oven to 350°F. Place the turkey meat side up in a 9x13-inch baking dish. Arrange the red potatoes around the turkey. Mix the broth and garlic in a medium mixing bowl. Pour over the turkey and potatoes. Sprinkle with the salt-free seasoning blend. Bake, covered, for 1 hour; remove the cover. Bake for 15 to 20 minutes longer or until a meat thermometer inserted in the thickest part of the turkey registers 170°F. Remove the turkey to a serving platter. Let stand, covered, for 10 minutes before carving. Yield: 8 servings

Per Serving: Calories 303; Fat 1 g; Sodium 133 mg; Dietary Fiber 2 g

SPECIAL OCCASIONS

Broccoli with Lemon Sauce

2 pounds fresh broccoli, trimmed
6 ounces cream cheese, softened
6 tablespoons milk
1 tablespoon fresh lemon juice
1 teaspoon lemon zest
½ teaspoon ground ginger
½ teaspoon cardamom
½ cup slivered almonds
1 tablespoon butter or margarine

Preheat the oven to 350°F. Combine the broccoli with a small amount of water in a 4-quart saucepan. Cook over medium-high heat for 7 minutes or until tender-crisp; drain. Arrange the broccoli in a greased 9x13-inch baking dish. Combine the cream cheese, milk, lemon juice, lemon zest, ginger and cardamom in a large mixer bowl. Beat at medium-high speed until smooth, scraping the bowl occasionally. Spoon over the broccoli. Bake for 15 minutes or until bubbly. Sauté the almonds in the butter in a small skillet until golden brown. Sprinkle over the broccoli. Yield: 6 servings

Per Serving: Calories 237; Fat 19 g; Sodium 153 mg; Dietary Fiber 6 g

Harvest Stuffing

1 cup chopped celery
⅔ cup chopped onion
⅔ cup butter or margarine
2½ teaspoons poultry seasoning
    Salt and pepper to taste
10 cups bread cubes
½ cup golden raisins
1 unpeeled large apple, chopped
½ cup chopped almonds, toasted
1½ cups chicken broth

Preheat the oven to 325°F. Sauté the celery and onion in the butter in a 10-inch skillet until tender. Stir in the poultry seasoning, salt and pepper. Remove from heat. Toss the bread cubes, raisins, apple and almonds in a large mixing bowl. Stir in the celery mixture. Add the broth and mix well. Spoon into a 5-quart baking pan. Bake for 1 hour or until brown and crisp. Yield: 10 servings

Per Serving: Calories 316; Fat 18 g; Sodium 463 mg; Dietary Fiber 4 g

SPECIAL OCCASIONS

Pumpkin Cheesecake

Crust
- 3 tablespoons butter or margarine
- 1 cup graham cracker crumbs
- 3 tablespoons sugar

Pumpkin Filling
- 16 ounces cream cheese, softened
- ¾ cup sugar
- 1 (15-ounce) can solid-pack pumpkin
- 1 teaspoon ground cinnamon
- ¼ teaspoon ground ginger
- ¼ teaspoon ground nutmeg
- 3 eggs

Topping
- 2 cups sour cream
- ¼ cup sugar
- 1 teaspoon vanilla extract
- Frozen whipped topping, thawed (optional)
- Chopped pecans or walnuts (optional)

Preheat the oven to 350°F. Coat the bottom and side of a 10-inch springform pan with vegetable oil. For the crust, microwave the butter in a medium microwave-safe dish on High for 30 to 60 seconds or until melted. Add the graham cracker crumbs and sugar and mix well. Pat the crumb mixture over the bottom of the prepared pan. For the filling, combine the cream cheese and sugar in a medium mixer bowl. Beat at medium-high speed until creamy, scraping the bowl occasionally. Add the pumpkin, cinnamon, ginger and nutmeg and mix well. Add the eggs 1 at a time, beating until blended after each addition. Spoon into the prepared crust. Bake for 50 minutes. Remove the pan to a wire rack. Increase the oven temperature to 400°F. For the topping, mix the sour cream, sugar and vanilla in a medium mixing bowl. Spread the sour cream mixture evenly over the top of the cheesecake. Bake for 8 minutes longer. Cool to room temperature on a wire rack. Run a sharp knife around the outer edge to loosen the cheesecake; remove the side. Chill, covered, for 4 hours to overnight. Garnish with whipped topping and pecans. Yield: 12 servings

Per Serving: Calories 389; Fat 26 g; Sodium 239 mg; Dietary Fiber 2 g

MENU

HOLIDAY COOKIE EXCHANGE

Since many of these cookies are so easy to make, why not gather a group of friends for a cookie exchange? Besides sampling them, part of the fun is giving them away.

Almond Biscotti

1½ cups all-purpose flour
1 teaspoon baking powder
¼ teaspoon salt
½ cup chopped almonds
½ cup sugar
2 eggs
1 teaspoon vanilla extract
½ teaspoon almond extract

Preheat the oven to 350°F. Mix the flour, baking powder and salt in a medium mixing bowl. Stir in the almonds. Combine the sugar and eggs in a medium mixer bowl. Beat at medium speed until blended. Stir in the flavorings. Add the flour mixture gradually, beating well after each addition. Shape the dough with lightly floured hands into 2 short logs. Arrange the logs on a cookie sheet lined with greased foil. Bake for 20 minutes. Cool to room temperature. Cut into 1-inch slices with a serrated knife. Arrange cut side down on a cookie sheet lined with foil. Bake for 20 minutes longer or until light brown. Remove to a wire rack to cool. Store in an airtight container for up to 2 days. Yield: 18 cookies

Per Serving: Calories 89; Fat 3 g; Sodium 67 mg; Dietary Fiber 1 g

Jam Thumbprints

½ cup butter or margarine, softened
⅓ cup sugar
1 egg yolk
1 teaspoon vanilla extract
1⅓ cups all-purpose flour
¼ cup any flavor jam, jelly or marmalade
⅓ cup slivered blanched almonds

Preheat the oven to 350°F. Beat the butter in a medium mixer bowl at high speed until light and fluffy. Add the sugar, beating constantly until blended. Add the egg yolk and vanilla and mix well. Add the flour gradually, beating constantly until blended. (The dough will be very firm.) Shape rounded teaspoonfuls of dough into balls. Place 2 inches apart on an ungreased cookie sheet. Make a deep indentation in the center of each cookie with thumb. Bake for 8 to 10 minutes or until firm. Remove from oven. Fill each indentation with ½ teaspoon of the jam. Sprinkle the jam with the almonds. Bake for 8 to 12 minutes longer or until light brown. Cool on the cookie sheet for 2 to 3 minutes. Remove the cookies to a wire rack to cool completely. Yield: 24 cookies

Per Serving: Calories 92; Fat 5 g; Sodium 41 mg; Dietary Fiber <1 g

SPECIAL OCCASIONS

Pecan Balls

1 cup butter or margarine, softened
½ cup sugar
2 teaspoons vanilla extract
2 cups all-purpose flour
1½ cups finely chopped pecans
¾ cup confectioners' sugar

Preheat the oven to 300°F. Combine the butter and sugar in a large mixer bowl. Beat at medium speed until light and fluffy, scraping the bowl occasionally. Add the vanilla, beating until blended. Add the flour and pecans gradually, beating well after each addition. Shape into balls, using a small scoop. Arrange 1 inch apart on an ungreased cookie sheet. Bake for 18 to 20 minutes or just until the cookies begin to brown around the edges. Cool on the cookie sheet for 2 to 3 minutes. Remove to a wire rack to cool slightly. Sprinkle the warm cookies with the confectioners' sugar. Yield: 42 cookies

Per Serving: Calories 106; Fat 7 g; Sodium 45 mg; Dietary Fiber <1 g

Twinkling Gingerbread Stars

1 (15-ounce) package gingerbread cake
   and cookie mix
24 assorted ring-shape hard candies,
   paper removed

Preheat the oven to 375°F. Prepare the gingerbread mix using the package directions for cookies. Divide the dough into 2 equal portions. Shape each portion into a ball. Roll each portion ⅛ inch thick on a lightly floured surface. Cut the dough with a star cutter. Arrange the dough stars carefully on a greased cookie sheet. Cut a circle of dough from the center of each cookie. Place one candy in each center. (Candies will melt and give a stained glass effect.) Bake for 10 minutes. Cool on the cookie sheet for 5 minutes. Remove to a wire rack to cool completely. Yield: 24 cookies

Per Serving: Calories 103; Fat 3 g; Sodium 128 mg; Dietary Fiber <1 g

SPECIAL OCCASIONS

MENU

HANUKKAH
CANDLE-LIGHTING PARTY

This celebration of light, combined with good food and family traditions,
helps create fond holiday memories.

Hummus with Tomato Relish   p.22

Sweet and Savory Beef Brisket   p.211

Sweet Potato Latkes   p.212

Cinnamon Applesauce   p.213

Snow-Capped Butter Balls   p.214

Sweet and Savory Beef Brisket

1 envelope onion soup mix, divided
1 (2-pound) beef brisket
2 tablespoons light brown sugar
1 tablespoon lemon zest
1 teaspoon ground cinnamon
1 teaspoon pepper
¾ teaspoon ground ginger
1½ cups apple juice
¼ cup honey
2 tablespoons orange marmalade
1 teaspoon Worcestershire sauce
1 (8-ounce) package dried apricots, chopped
1 cup chopped pitted prunes
8 ounces noodles, cooked, drained

Preheat the oven to 350°F. Line a large roasting pan with foil. Sprinkle half the soup mix over the bottom of the roasting pan. Add the brisket. Rub the remaining soup mix into the brisket. Bring the edges of the foil over the brisket and seal tightly. Bake for 3 hours. Combine the brown sugar, lemon zest, cinnamon, pepper and ginger in a medium mixing bowl and mix well. Stir in the apple juice, honey, orange marmalade and Worcestershire sauce. Add the apricots and prunes and mix well. Open the foil carefully. Pour the fruit mixture over the brisket and reseal. Bake for 1 hour longer or until the brisket is tender. Serve over hot cooked noodles. Yield: 6 servings

Per Serving: Calories 710; Fat 12 g; Sodium 682 mg; Dietary Fiber 9 g

SPECIAL OCCASIONS

Sweet Potato Latkes

1 pound sweet potatoes or yams, peeled, shredded
2 tablespoons minced fresh ginger root
½ cup whole milk or 2% milk
½ cup all-purpose flour
2 eggs
1 tablespoon sugar
1 teaspoon baking powder
1 teaspoon salt
Vegetable oil for frying

Mix the sweet potatoes and ginger root in a large mixing bowl. Combine the milk, flour, eggs, sugar, baking powder and salt in a blender container or food processor. Process just until mixed. Add to the sweet potato mixture and mix well. Add oil to a 12-inch skillet to measure ½ inch. Heat to 365°F. Drop ⅓ cup of the sweet potato batter into the hot oil for each pancake. Cook for 3 to 4 minutes or until golden brown on the bottom; turn. Cook for 3 to 4 minutes longer; drain. Serve with Cinnamon Applesauce on page 213. Yield: 10 pancakes

Per Serving: Calories 79; Fat 2 g; Sodium 303 mg; Dietary Fiber 1 g

Nutritional information does not include oil for frying.

Cinnamon Applesauce

4 pounds baking apples, cored
1 lemon, cut into quarters, seeded
  Red hot cinnamon candies to taste
½ cup apple juice, apple cider or water
  Honey or maple syrup to taste

Peel the apples if desired and cut into quarters. Combine the apples, lemon and cinnamon candies in a large heavy stockpot. Add the apple juice. Bring to a boil over medium-high heat; reduce heat. Simmer, covered, over low heat for 20 minutes or until the apples are tender, stirring occasionally and adding more apple juice if needed. Put the apple mixture through a food mill using the preferred blade. Add the desired amount of honey or maple syrup and mix well. Chill, covered, until serving time. Yield: 8 servings

Per Serving: Calories 120; Fat 1 g; Sodium 1 mg; Dietary Fiber 4 g

SPECIAL OCCASIONS

Snow-Capped Butter Balls

2 cups sifted all-purpose flour
½ teaspoon salt
1 cup butter or margarine, softened
½ cup superfine sugar
2 teaspoons vanilla extract
½ cup sifted confectioners' sugar
(optional)

Preheat the oven to 325°F. Sift the flour and salt together. Combine the butter and superfine sugar in a medium mixer bowl. Beat at medium-high speed until light and fluffy, scraping the bowl occasionally. Add the vanilla and mix well. Add the flour mixture gradually, beating well after each addition. Chill, covered, for 1 to 2 hours. Shape the dough into 1-inch balls. Arrange 2 inches apart on an ungreased cookie sheet. Bake for 15 minutes or until light brown. Cool on the cookie sheet for 2 minutes. Remove to a wire rack to cool completely. Roll each cookie in the confectioners' sugar. Yield: 48 cookies

Per Serving: Calories 59; Fat 4 g; Sodium 63 mg; Dietary Fiber <1 g

Index

Index

Index

Index

Index

Index

Italian Basil Shrimp, 62
Italian Vegetable Kabobs, 119

J
Jam Thumbprints, 207

K
Kiwifruit
  Kiwi Lime Pie, 159
  Minty Fruit Bowl, 183
  Spinach and Raspberry Salad, 106
  Tropical Fruit Salsa, 28

L
Layered Mexican Bean Dip, 23
Lemon Carrots, 115
Lemon Cheese Coffee Cake, 87
Low-Fat Cinnamon Apple
    Muffins, 91
Lucky Leek Soup, 174

M
Magical Biscuits, 85
Mediterranean-Style Pasta Salad, 111
Melon Salad with Orange Lime
    Dressing, 191

Menus
  Easter Buffet, 179
  Father's Day, 186
  4th of July Potluck, 189
  Hanukkah Candle-Lighting Party, 210
  Holiday Cookie Exchange, 205
  Mother's Day, 182
  New Year's Eve, 165
  Pumpkin Carving, 195
  Saint Patrick's Day Dinner, 173
  Thanksgiving Feast, 200
  Valentine's Day, 169
Merry Berry Syrup, 92
Mexican Munch, 34
Mexican Taco Pie, 50
Minty Fruit Bowl, 183
Mock Champagne, 168
Monterey Strata, 78
Muffins
  Low-Fat Cinnamon Apple Muffins, 91
  Soda Bread Muffins, 178
Mushrooms
  Angel Hair Pasta with Vegetables, 121
  Beef and Spring Vegetables with Pasta, 45
  Breakfast Pie, 75
  Fresh Mushroom Salad, 104

Gingery Rice Pilaf, 124
Italian Basil Shrimp, 62
Italian Vegetable Kabobs, 119
Mushroom Puffs, 18
Shrimp and Swiss Frittata, 79
Steak Diane, 170
Stuffed Mushroom Spinach Pizza, 72

N
North Stars, 166
Nutty Pineapple Slaw, 107

O
Old-Fashioned Apple Bread Pudding, 130
Orange
  Autumn Fruit Salad, 102
  Breakfast Blizzard, 36
  Honey Spiced Tea, 38
  Melon Salad with Orange
    Lime Dressing, 191
  Orange Cream Fruit Salad, 101
  Rainbow Fruit Cups, 136
  Red Velvet Punch, 37
  Summer Fruit Soup, 82
  Sunshine Grits, 83
  Sweet Potato Salad, 109

Index

Index

Index

Index